Paid To Poop

Other books by Brad Myers:

Nope, no other books yet. You let me know if I should.

Other work by Brad Myers:

Visit my website here: http://www.paidtopoop.org

Enjoy my blog here: http://paidtopoop.blogspot.com/

Paid To Poop

A Humorous Look at Work and How to Avoid It

By Brad Myers

Copyright © 2012 by Brad Myers. All rights reserved.

bradmyers@paidtopoop.org

www.paidtopoop.org

All Rights Reserved. No part of this publication may be reproduced, distributed, or transmitted in any form or by any means, including photocopying, recording, or other electronic or mechanical methods, without the prior written permission of the author.

Crappy Tables and Hand Drawn Junk (except the cool cartoon) by Brad Myers

Cover design by Michael Ballard
Cool cartoon by Dave Carleson

First Edition, 2012
I'm Sorry

ISBN-13: 978-0-9855918-0-9 (Brad\Myers)
ISBN-10: 0985591803

"For Pottery Girl"

Acknowledgements

Without Gwen, nothing happens – anywhere in my world. Regardless of how poorly written, unorganized, and questionable the content; finishing this would never have happened without your love and support. And to everyone else in my life because without you… I'm not funny.

Contents

Preface 9

Chapter 1: APE Interviews 15

Chapter 2: A Real APE Situation 24

Chapter 3: Job Difficulty and Their Level of Expectations 33

Chapter 4: OOA 45

Chapter 5: Pretty People 49

Chapter 6: Answering Email 53

Chapter 7: Texting 69

Chapter 8: The Potty Protocol 74

Chapter 9: Bathroom Babble 103

Chapter 10: Paid to Poop 115

Chapter 11: The End 134

Preface

Don't worry, your money was well spent – I spent it on liquor, Bugle cones, and canned cheese. But you do have a nice book here, so I hope you enjoy it. Contrary to what the obvious title implies, this book isn't just about bathrooms and what you get to do in there. It's about office life and getting through it with humor. It provides tips on interviewing and how to handle different personalities in the work place and even has a chapter as a self-help guide on how to respond to electronic mail (email). It teaches proper bathroom etiquette in the choices you should make and what you can say, and what you should avoid saying completely. In all cases, use my tips tailored by your better judgment.

I'll admit that it's openly biased toward men and I am sorry about that. But I am not legally allowed in the women's bathroom and previous incarceration for violating that has led me to be a little gun shy of field research. So all of my work has been in men's bathrooms and conducting interviews in those bathrooms to give you the information you deserve – no matter how creepy that seems.

This short book will walk you through office logistics and protocols to provide you with things to try to make your office experience more enjoyable. Failing that, I've ensured that each chapter can be read in about the same amount of time it might take you to finish pooping (save the chapter on "Answering Email" for a morning after tequila and chili; you'll have extra time). Each chapter is written in the way I try to run my life; half-assed and out of order. I kept it short to save both of us time, and you money – so you're really the winner in all of this.

I don't consider myself an authority on work or pooping but I have done them both for most of my life so I am proficient. But the opinions and expressions along with the insults and racism you are about to read are meant to be funny and not cruel. Having said that, I believe that if someone starts out by saying:

"I don't mean to offend ..."

They are actually about to offend you. They say that first and feel it'll soften the blow just before they do actually offend you. It's the same principle as someone telling you this:

"To be honest ..."

That just means they were previously lying to you. I'm not apologizing for offending anyone in this book, but I'm sure someone is going to take offense. I'm just asking them to realize that everything in the world is funny, even stereotypes, midgets, and forty-five year old white guys with small penises and a need to be accepted. In all cases, I'm trying to be funny- not offensive. If you find something offensive then it probably is to you, but it was funny to someone else. I never wrote anything with the intent on being offensive. So, if you are offended by anything, <u>I'm sorry you feel that way</u> and you might try lightening up on your self-view; it'll make your life "fun-nier." You don't have much time on Earth to waste any of it mad at someone stupid like me. I'm not mad at you.

I do hope you enjoy it and can get past anything offensive—If it makes you feel any better, I had to get past some offensive things just to write and publish this thing, like these:

- 💩 If you're reading this on a Kindle or some other newfangled smart gadget, the formatting might seem goofy or off. You may see some oddness with bulleted lists, charts, and other things that just aren't my fault. The content is all my fault, but the funky formatting might not be. Try making the text smaller on your

- 💩 Kindle or favorite screen reader – until you can't see it anymore and then request your money back.

- 💩 I felt offensive, but mostly hypocritical, that I didn't write any of this book while pooping.

- 💩 This isn't about being offended so it's not related to what I'm talking about right now, but I don't discuss animals and their bathroom habits at all. Or at least I don't think I do, and I'm not going to proofread any more, I'm tired of that. I only mention animals aren't mentioned because I don't want any animals offended and then contacting me.

- 💩 While I understand why I can't sit in a women's bathroom for three hours performing my research, I did find it offensive to be kicked and slapped when I asked women about their bathroom behavior. Therefore, there is a gross lack of any details for my female readers, but that's also your own fault... so there. Let me in!

People waste a lot of energy on finding things to be upset about, this book shouldn't be on your list, it's just not worth it. I hope you understand that it's just simple crude humor created by a simple crude individual. However, I do encourage any and all comments that you care to share, so please find my email address on the copyright page and let me know how you feel.

If you do use any of my tips on interviewing, or apply my techniques on answering email, I'd love for you to share that with me so I can post it on my blog. If you have stories of Potty Protocol breaches or real world experience using the

Apply, Prepare, Excite (APE) approach to interviews, I'd be grateful if you shared them.

I'm driven by humor and making people laugh- it's my drug. I encourage comments and appreciate feedback. I truly hope you do enjoy my attempt at office humor and can relate to at least some of it. Thank you for purchasing my book, now go on in, sit down and enjoy yourself and get Paid to Poop.

Chapter 1:

APE Interviews

"*You're fired!*" It's a miserable way to learn that you suck at what you do, isn't it? It's the work force equivalent of being told to f*** off without someone actually saying those words. Whether you're fired, laid off, or the victim of a restructuring, it all means the same thing; you'll soon be looking for another job.

Interviewing for a job can be one of the most stressful things you'll ever do. Job interviews expose you to scrutiny, force you to change your routine, and make you uncomfortable– much like diarrhea. In this current economic downturn where job loss is happening faster than house values are falling, you might think this is no laughing matter. But I will always contend that no matter how bad it gets, if you aren't laughing at something, you're dead inside and it's showing on your outside.

Ok, so you've been fired; lift yourself up, get cleaned up, and grab a book to help you find another job – but not this book – this book is supposed to make you laugh. Finish reading this book and then go grab a real self-help book on job interviews and get your resume polished. When you're ready to interview, read the literature on interviewing – again, not this literature – read my stuff to make you laugh and have some fun, that way everything else will fall into place.

I've put together a short and simple method for approaching job interviews that I apply when interviewing. I interview a lot because I rarely land a job, so I'm pretty good at interviewing, just not good at getting a job.

Your resume is your entire life's work on one or two type-written pages, broken into sections such as Work History, Experience, Education, Skills, and Interests. It's the first impression prospective employers are going to use to determine if they want you to come in for an interview. Your resume is very important and it has to capture their attention. So, even if you were someone who received these overused statements in grade school:

"A pleasure to have in my class"

Or,

"Works well with others"

You still have to polish your resume to impress prospective employers. In the work force; sharing your crayons and faking like you're polite can only get you so far. Although those are nice comments that a lazy grade school teacher once lied to you about, they don't translate very well in the real world. Sure, you need to be liked and "a pleasure" and work well with other people, but that's a baseline for getting a job – you need skills and a plan above that for today's job interviews.

The interviewer has a small amount of time to judge you and to assess whether you are a good fit for his or her company. They're judging how you sit, speak, look, and smell. You might have to sit there for an hour or more, sweating, fidgeting, and nearly crapping yourself for a job you really didn't want in the first place. Job interviews can be stressful –

even painful – but if you're comfortable and happy, your chance for success increases.

Job interviews are fun, if you make them that way. I don't have a list of tips, hints, or tricks that will make you interview well – you should Google that – but I can show you a few things I consider when I interview for jobs. They might help, they might hinder, but if you follow my lead you can make your interviews more relaxing and fun without the troublesome burden of receiving a callback. I call this my **APE** approach to interviews.

1. **Apply**
2. **Prepare**
3. **Excite**

1. Apply for a job you are going to like.

Telling a jobless guy that he "needs to apply" is the same as telling sales people to ask for the sale at the end of the pitch. If you don't ask, you won't get the sale. Same for applying for a job; if you don't apply, you won't get the interview, and without the interview; you can't get the job. So make sure you are applying for something you want to do because you might actually get it. The one thing that leads to a successful interview before you even start is to apply for something you really like to do.

You should be excited and happy about the job you are applying for. If you are, you're more likely to show your excitement and interest with facial expressions, attitude, and body posture during the interview. People like happy people. Having passion for what you want to do helps you be successful. Pick a job that you can handle and will enjoy doing for years to come. But you have to be careful. For instance, I love rockets but I'm stupid so I can't be a Rocket Scientist. I like fire, but I don't like living with men so I can't be a Fireman. But there are exceptions, like this one: I like to write, I'm not good at it, but if you're reading this then at least I sold something. Boo-ya! Apply for something you find interesting and/or fun.

Sometimes it's very difficult to find a job we like but we still must find a job. This is when we start settling for what's available and that can be tragic because you find yourself working in a union for some huge airplane manufacturer making a good living where you're likely to stay for your entire working career. Those are the most difficult interviews because you really don't want the job, yet it's probably the most stable thing you'll ever have. If you are settling for a job you don't want, you still have to enter the interview happy and energetic. You can't go in with the corners of your mouth flat, your arms draped at your side and cinder blocks for hands – you'll look pathetic. And none of us want pathetic looking, sad people building our airplanes.

When you apply for a job you don't necessarily want, it doesn't mean you have to take the job when/if they offer you one. But if you can hold out for a position like "stunt dick" for pornography films, then do that – definitely do that. Otherwise, be sure to apply for something you are going to like doing – failing that, you can fall back on the jobs you have to settle for.

2. **Prepare** well.

You should research the position as well as the company you plan to interview with. It gives you insight on the direction the company is headed and what your role and responsibilities might be. Read their website and become familiar with mission statements, directives, and any other managerial crap because you may need to regurgitate it during the interview. Websites sometimes have hot business chicks smiling or doing some other sexy pose to entice and allure viewers. It's eye candy. Nobody who looks like that actually works at that company – it just doesn't happen – unless you're applying for a towel boy position at a high-end brothel. So even if their web site shows hot chicks; always imagine shorter, uglier, and smaller breasted women working there. That way you'll be pleasantly surprised if you get the job and the women are one out of three of those things; like short and ugly but has big tits. That's the real world and life is about tradeoffs, my friend. Anyway, by empowering yourself with knowledge of your target company, you can prepare to make specific, pertinent statements during the interview process. For example, you may need to throw out a statement like this:

You: *"I read that your company has a recent patent on widget test tools allowing you to realize an increase in productivity of 25%. That's pretty impressive."*

This statement shows that you've done your homework and understood specific data about their company. You've also managed to compliment their business and that's a step in the right direction for a successful interview. But that's really not what I'm writing about in this chapter. I want you to have fun in your interview and raise some eyebrows. I want you to ask real questions that you want real answers to. Take the web site example I used earlier about showing hot chicks working there; you want to know about the people that actually work there compared to the ones they show on their web site. A more pertinent question to ask that won't get you the job but will force a reaction would be:

You: *"So, why is the actual woman at the receptionist desk nothing like the woman on your web site? The woman on your web site has nice breasts, but the woman in the reception* *area only has nice posture. Would I be working with the woman who has nice breasts?"*

Yes, it's sexual harassment of some sort, and piggish by all means, I get that. But I feel they harassed me by displaying false advertisement on their web site. If you can't find that person at their place of business then it's a lie. You're just asking an important question related to their web site and your potential employment.

To prepare well, you will have researched the company, browsed their web site, and reviewed financial statements, if needed. Perhaps you've even spoken with a few employees. There's no harm in being relaxed during the interview and enjoying yourself while finding out if there are any hot chicks working there. You should want to find out all information prior to accepting a position and/or potentially using that information in your defense hearing for sexual harassment.

Always prepare well for your interview. It makes you more comfortable during the process and being comfortable makes you more confident. Being confident and landing a new job can be rewarding and exciting. This brings me to the "E" in my APE approach to interviews.

3. Excite. Be excited about the interview.

Applying for a job you like and being prepared are good steps toward a successful interview. Being excited about the interview is equally important as it shows your enthusiasm about their company and the position you are applying for. If you've applied for a job you like, and you've prepared well, then getting excited is just a progression of those first two steps. However, if it's a job you're really excited about, take the extra step and spend a few minutes in the parking lot working up a minor boner prior to the interview.

Read on, it's not entirely what you're thinking. You'll feel more confident, excited, willing, and ready to perform. They'll see your enthusiasm in your face and in your pants. Plus, your chances of landing the job, a date, and even incarceration have increased significantly. So prepare for your job interview both mentally and physically; show your excitement!

If you were interviewing for a job you really wanted, like strip club DJ, or oil boy for a supermodel runway ramp, then you'd be energetic, excited, and should be sporting about 75% chub prior to the interview. The interview would be a snap:

Lucky Strip Club Owner Guy: *"Do you like girls?"*

You: *"Yep."*

Lucky Strip Club Owner Guy: *"Do you like music?"*

You: *"Yep."*

Lucky Strip Club Owner Guy: *"Are you excited about working at a place like this?"*

You: *"Can't you tell?"*

Ok, so maybe it is exactly what you were thinking, but there seems to be negative connotation with having boners at job interviews and I'm trying to change that. A man should be proud when he's at attention, but in today's society, people point and laugh at ~~me~~you. For women, that "glow-about-your-face" you have after a romp shows satisfaction, pride, and confidence – it's beautiful and you know it. Being proud, confident, and beautiful are important qualities in any interview. It's about feeling your best, displaying your best, and interviewing with a smile. So before your next interview, men should work up a stiffy in the parking lot and women should try to "sink the little man in the boat," you'll be more excited and they might find the awkwardness appealing.

💩 💩 💩

Given the right attitude and proper physical preparation, most interviews can be fun and exciting. Technology interviews are my favorite because everyone is so smart – or they're supposed to be. But it's important to remember that in every college class, someone had to finish last. There is always one person who isn't the sharpest tool in the shed. Just like you have a jackass or more in your work place, they can be found in other work places too. For example, you might not think so but even in the cockpit of the Space Shuttle, one of those people is the dimmest bulb. He's farting in space helmets before liftoff, pratfalling on important switches, and does rock-paper-scissors to see who uses the shitter first. Not all doctors, astronauts, and strip club owners are the smartest people.

In the technology industry, there seems to be more smart people than there are dumb people, but that's because of all the Asians. (I know, I know – racial profiling – but like I discuss in a later chapter on email; Asians are smarter than you, so just accept it). But you should realize that sometimes, the interviewer who's pointing out that your rock polishing hobby seems "fascinating," might just be a dolt who loves shiny rocks and isn't qualified to interview you. But that's rarely the case, so you need to watch out for yourself – there really are smarter people than you in the world.

It might be comforting to realize that the person interviewing you is nearly retarded and in charge of hiring, but that's not your best scenario. If you passed the interview and took the job, how long until this hiring manager realizes s/he's got competition for "weakest link" and ousts you? So if you are in an interview where the person doing the hiring is dumber than you, it's really not a good fit. Sure, it seems enticing to be in a position where your minimal efforts are perceived as exceptional. But someday you're going to have to be accountable for those efforts and may even be asked to reproduce them. That stuff is for the "Go-Getters" (I also explain Go-Getters in a later chapter, I think this is called "foreshadowing").

When faced with an interview situation where you start to feel like you're a star – like this company would actually benefit from you being there – get the hell out! You won't be comfortable at a job where you're expected to work every day for at least eight hours AND produce tangible, measurable results. It's just not a good fit. In interviews where you get that impression, adjust your boner, and excuse yourself from the interview with;

> *"I'm sorry, but I'm not going to waste this on the likes of you."*

To sum up your interview preparation, be an **APE**:

- **A**pply for a job you like.
- **P**repare well for the interview and the potential position.
- **E**xcite yourself for confidence and pleasure. Enter the interview with a boner or having worked yourself over in the parking lot.

To help you see how this process is deployed, the following chapter shows you an example of an interview I went on and applied the APE approach. It's an example of a real interview and real situations. You can do this too, it's not weird. So be confident and proud, wear your best clothes, show your stuff and have fun...You'll be glad you did.

Chapter 2:

A Real APE Situation

Although my **APE** approach is fun, it is also incredibly effective as I'm sure you can see. However, I would recommend that you consider some actual training and help with your resume. If implemented incorrectly, my approach might land you in jail or curled up in a gutter after being beaten by ugly people. Better to be safe and use the Internet to find yourself some useable information. I'd like to share a mostly true story to help illustrate my **APE** approach to interviews. This was a job interview I had with a technology company several years ago:

Using my **APE** approach, I **A**pplied for a job I thought I'd like, it was SomeTechCompany and they made banking software. Actually, I knew I wouldn't like it but since my application for Dressing Room Cleaner for Victoria's Secret modeling room was rejected, I decided to settle. I don't recommend you ever settle for what you don't like, I'm just weak and fat and lazy. Anyway, I **P**repared for the possibility of an interview by researching this technology firm and Victoria's Secret web site, just in case. After that type of preparation I was also **E**xcited and I hadn't even received a callback yet! You see? It's already been a winning situation for me. Anyway, I was cleaning up when the phone rang...

Me: *"Hello."*

Tom the Tech Guy: *"Hello is Jib Carrib home?"*

Me: *"Yes, this is he."*

Tom the Tech Guy: *"Great! Hello Mr. Carrib, I'm Tom from SomeTechCompany and I've reviewed your application and would love to meet you for an interview. Does Tuesday at two o'clock work for you?"*

Me: *"That's great, sure Tuesday at two works for me... But do you guys work every Tuesday?"*

Tom the Tech Guy: *"Um, yes, yes we do. Will that be a problem if you were to be hired?"*

Me: *"Not for <u>me</u>, no."*

Tom the Tech Guy: *"Oh. Ok, well why don't you come down on Tuesday and we'll discuss some things and I'll have you meet your partner in QA whom you'd be working with. She's blah, blah, blah ..."*

He didn't actually say, "...blah, blah, blah" he was describing what she did or something. Hell, he might have said she gives hand jobs at lunch and makes sandwiches in addition to running the QA department, but I never heard anything because I tuned out as soon as he said *"She's ..."* I just knew this person wasn't going to look like anyone on their web site or at Victoria's Secret. But I'd already agreed to do the interview, so I had to go. I was going to make the best of it and have fun. Besides, who knew, maybe I'd be surprised...But I wouldn't be writing about this if I had been.

Tom the Tech Guy: *"... So, can I expect to see you at two o'clock on Tuesday?"*

Me: *"Sure, I'll be excited."*

Tuesday came quicker than I wanted it to; I still hadn't wrapped up my final quest in a video game that I had over fifty hours into but I was sure to finish after the interview. I showered and shaved and hopped into my Pinto and drove to Some Tech Company. I stopped at the AM/PM mini-mart and picked up three Red Bulls, a package of chewy Spree's, and one of my favorite magazines. I arrived thirty minutes early for the interview and found a distant parking spot shaded by a beautiful cherry blossom tree. I popped a Bull, took a swig and perused the magazine – thirty minutes was plenty. The "articles" were amazing. I prepared a little more for the interview by concentrating on the magazine articles. I drank the other two Bulls and exited the Pinto in slight discomfort but also excited.

On the long walk to the front door, I popped four Spree's into my mouth to freshen my breath. I couldn't help focusing on the girl I might be working with. This was a technology job and I've worked in the technology industry for a while and the hottest test engineer ever was an eight out of ten. However, that's a tech-troll eight meaning she was really a three or an ugly four outside the office doors. So the girl I'm about to meet already has an advantage – she's new and different – some strange, you know what I mean? Unfortunately, I was too focused on wondering what she was going to look like and started to lose my chub.

I was fifteen feet from the entrance doors and wired on Bulls and Spree's and I had a fading boner. I had to act fast. I grabbed for my cell phone and acted like I was taking a call. I turned away from the doors and started to think about the cover girl on my magazine. But that didn't work because she was *so* ten minutes ago. We're all pigs. I turned a bit toward the door, still fake-talking, to see if anyone was watching – All clear.

I turned back from the door and realized my cheap pants were a bit tight in my junk area and created a bit of friction each time I twisted at the waist. So I spent the next five minutes fake-talking and twisting back and forth until I built up a nice friction boner. The **APE** was complete. I headed in.

> **Me:** *"Hi, I'm Jib Carrib, I'm here for an interview with Tom."*
>
> **Not the Hot Receptionist from their Web Site:** *"Sure, I'll let him know you're here. Please, have a seat."*
>
> **Me:** *"Thanks, I'd better stand."*

I met Tom and went into his office and we started chatting about the weather and the Seattle Seahawks before diving into the interview. He asked me about the software lifecycle and I regurgitated what I read about that the night before. It sounded great and the interview was going well, I felt comfortable and Tom seemed pleased. I was excited and cheerful and amped up on Bulls and Spree's so I don't remember a lot of what was said but I do remember meeting the girl.

Tom hit his speaker phone and called her over. She came to the door of the office while I was discussing defect reduction goals and their importance in achieving solid perceived quality (I don't even know what the hell that means). Tom acknowledged her over my shoulder, so I respectfully stood and turned to greet her.

Yep, she was large all right, just like I expected. She stood in the doorway waving her hand in a friendly "Hello" gesture – her one toothed grin beaming. That wasn't a misprint; she had only one front tooth. The three of us stood there in awkward silence until Tom realized that she was actually stuck in the door jamb and motioning for help. As professional-looking as a manager can be while prying an employee from a door jamb, he helped her into the room.

Fat Tech-Troll: *"Sorry... that rarely happens."* She lied.

Tom the Tech Guy: *"You know, they just don't build office door frames like they used to."* He said, trying to ease the situation. *"They're a lot more narrow nowadays – probably saves trees."*

He was trying to be nice and "politically correct" (pc) which is just an oxymoron; it's just a two word term for "lying." Political and correct should always go together but they never have and never will except when explaining that things should be politically correct – circular logic. The fact is that she's too fat for the door if she chooses to walk through it head on. If she shimmied and shuffled sideways through the door then she'd probably fit a little better.

Instead of having a good laugh at an obviously funny situation; she was embarrassed, I felt awkward, and he had to lie and treat her like a child. I stood there just biting my tongue hoping the pain would squelch the need to laugh. But all it did was soften my stiffy.

Tom the Tech Guy: *"Jib, this is Chris. Chris is our test lead on the project you'd be working on. Chris, this is Jib Carrib."*

Me: *"Hi Chris, it's nice to meet you."* I said, extending my hand for a firm handshake.

Lame! That was the only thing I could say in that situation. I couldn't say what I wanted to – which had the words "funny," "door," and "you" in it somewhere. But to be fair, fatness is relative because she wouldn't be fat if she were 8' tall. But since she was the same height as she was in width, and wore a plaid flannel shirt; she looked like a 4'6" tall Rubik's Cube. She waddled forward and I shook her claw.

Rubik's Cube: *"It's nice to meet you, too."*

She plopped herself on the sofa across from my chair, I sat back down but I couldn't stop stealing glances at her. In part because Tom kept talking about how nice of a personality she had but also because it was like watching the fat bearded lady at the circus and I couldn't avert my eyes. She was a hulk of a short woman and wore a black knitted skull cap that had "Harley-Chick" knitted in red across the brow.

Speaking of her brow, I expected two. I also expected less facial and ear hair on my potential female coworkers. I was impressed, however, that she didn't smell like moldy bread considering the food shards she brushed from her collar. She actually smelled pleasant, much like pickles and lettuce fallen from a burger, I suppose. I was getting hungry and my boner was gone. My attitude was going to hell and I wanted out of there. The last thing I wanted to do was offend anyone – because I don't do that – but I needed an out. Then she moved and grabbed a copy of my resume off of Tom's desk and read quietly for about thirty seconds. Then, she spoke:

Rubik's Cube: *"So, it says here you tested voice application software. What we do here is a lot different and more complicated and important I'm sure; but can you tell me what web language testing experience you've had?"*

Me: *"Our administration interface is browser based so I've been exposed to testing HTML, XHTML, ASP, XML, VBScript, Java, and JavaScript."*

Rubik's Cube: *"I also see here that you're a "quick learner." But what we really need is someone that already knows stuff. Are you someone that already knows stuff or am I going to have to teach you?"*

Me: *"Oh, well, I would expect a small learning curve, but I ..."*

Rubik's Cube: *"Never mind, I can tell there will be some training involved. I don't think he's a good fit Tom"* She injected and casually tossed my resume on the desk.

Tom the Tech Guy: *"Great, great to see some dialogue, but let's move forward with the interview. So Jib, you seem to have a great attitude and experience in testing. We have other candidates we need to interview but before you go do you have any questions for us?"*

You should always have questions at this point in the interview. Not having questions sends the message that you don't have any independent thoughts – which is a good thing while watching strippers on a pole, but not good during an interview. Make stuff up if you have to but ask questions about the company's strengths or their three to five year goals or any of that crap you don't really care about but you know they do. But I couldn't think of anything important to ask because I was flustered by the fat cube calling me stupid. However, in your interviews, you should avoid asking about salary unless one of two things happens:

1) The interviewer brings the topic up, or...
2) The fat lesbian just insulted you.

Me: *"Sure, I have a question, thanks... So Tom, how much do you make here?"*

Tom the Tech Guy: *"I'm sorry, we don't discuss salary during the interview."*

Me: *"Sure, ok. Then what kind of car do you drive to work every day?"*

Tom the Tech Guy: *"Look Jib, are these really the questions you want to end your interview on?"*

Me: *"No, no, I'm sorry, I just lost interest as soon as I saw the fat chick but I didn't want to be rude and just leave."*

Rubik's Cube: *"Fat!?!?"*

Me: *"You're not? ... Wait, big boned?"*

Tom the Tech Guy: *"That's it. You're outta here. Get out, now!"*

He stood up and came from around his desk and grabbed my arm as I stood. Rubik's Cube called me a pig as I was escorted out but I turned to her and apologized anyway. I thought she was pretty rude. Tom held the door open and told me not to call or come around the building ever again.

Me: *"Tom, I'm sorry, but Tuesday's just aren't my best day. Can we re-do this interview on Thursday?"*

Tom the Tech Guy: *"You're lucky I don't call the police."*

So I walked back to my car, drove home, and finished that final quest on my video game, making the day bitter sweet. I still didn't have a job, and finishing that video game was symbolic of my life in that I spent so much time playing that damn game that I didn't focus on landing a good job. Now that the game was over, and I had ruined a good chance at a secure future, I was sad and pathetic.

I sat in front of my computer and watched the game credits scroll by. All those people listed had good jobs, how did they get those? They're probably smart and more motivated to work than a masseur at a women's brothel. I realized that my life could be over, just like the game, if I didn't shape up and do something more productive. Perhaps I should use some of the suggestions I found on the Internet and get myself a good job with pay and benefits rather than playing video games all the time…

The last credit scrolled by and the screen faded to black. I sighed, opened a browser and searched on "fat lesbian lumberjacks" and clicked "images."

"*Holy crap- that's her!*"

Ziiippppp.

Chapter 3:

Job Difficulty and Their Level of Expectations

Unfortunately, we all can't work at strip clubs, so we have to find other jobs, maybe even ones we're not comfortable doing. People put higher expectations on your performance in jobs that are considered more difficult or require more education, experience, and/or training. That sounds fair, but what scale is used to determine how difficult one job is from the next? Also, do the expectations of good performance change with the difficulty of the job? Those are tough questions, but I have my own answers – and I bet they make perfect sense.

Generally speaking, people might base the difficulty of a particular job on the amount of formal education required to perform that job. For example, let's look at a brain surgeon vs. a waitress: Most would say that operating on a brain would be more difficult than waiting tables. But I'd argue differently – neither could trade places and be effective. Each given a week at the others job, the brain surgeon might figure out which check belongs to which table and may even take and deliver orders correctly by the end of the week. But who likes brain surgeons? They're cold, emotionless, arrogant, and have very little patience for stupid people, of which they think everyone else is.

The waitress might crack open her first brain and cut the right thing out, who knows? She might make a critical mistake and kill someone, but that's not because the job is difficult, it's only because of the lack of proper education. But any patient that did live would love her caring personality and attention to detail when it comes to working with individuals. (Note: There are very nice brain surgeons that aren't all those bad things I said, and there are shitty waitresses that probably should have been brain surgeons because of their horrific personality. Sorry about that low blow to any brain surgeons that read books like this. (Note to the Note: if your brain surgeon reads books like this one, you need a new brain surgeon)).

I've incredibly and effectively shown that a brain surgeons' job is just as difficult as a waitress' job. And that the major difference between professions is in the amount of proper education. You might argue that the eight years of education the brain surgeon went through was difficult. I'd remind you that we aren't talking about how each person got to their job – otherwise, I'd tell you that the waitress spent eight years serving burgers to dicks like you and selling blow to teenagers just to make ends meet, while her piece of shit boyfriend cheated on her relentlessly with her sister and mom. I think the brain surgeon can get his degree online at the University of Arrogance. The waitress gets hers from the College of Living, where there are no silver spoons.

Even though the difficulty is equal, you can clearly see that the level of expectations for each job might be drastically different. For the brain surgeon, his employer (which might be the hospital and the patient) expects surgeries to be performed to near perfection. Certainly the waitress has similar expectations placed on her as well; she has to get orders correct, smile while dirt-bags order crap that's not on the menu, and she must deliver drinks efficiently or someone gets pissed and doesn't leave a tip. The expectations of efficient performance are the same for the hospital and the restaurant: they want their brain surgeon and waitress to be productive at work. So the employers' expectations are pretty high that they do their job well.

But expectations are completely subjective. Expectations are literally something we anticipate to happen – they aren't always met, and they are not always what you "expect." I might expect different results from my brain surgeon than you would. Where you just want your surgery to go well and fix whatever you have broken in your brain, I expect the brain surgeon to tweak some stuff up there to give me super human strength or increased orgasms, something cool like that. You might expect your waitress to be quick and friendly, while I just expect her to have nice tits and not expect a huge tip.

So the difficulty of each job could be the same, but the expectations may be drastically different, depending on the perspective. When you're looking for work; police officer, bartender, firefighter, and waiter are all similar in their level of difficulty, but the level of expectations of you doing the job effectively may be different.

When you're interviewing for jobs as often as I do, you get pretty experienced at it…Not necessarily better at it, just more experienced. Understanding your own perception of what is "difficult" and what the "expectations" are on you to perform that job, will greatly increase your chance of getting that job and being happy with it. The more interviews you go on, the more experienced you'll get. I don't believe I interview very well – I think my personality puts people off… Who knew? I tend to smile a lot during interviews in part because I have the boner but also because you are supposed to look happy and interested in the position you are applying for. However, I lack many skills so I come off looking like a goofball. But I keep going on them because I make them fun and the experience is rewarding.

Regardless of your experience at interviewing, you probably feel that there are many jobs that you simply can't interview for based only on your lack of qualifications. I don't think this should stop you from trying, because all interviews are educational and fun, and remember: practice makes perfect. If you go on enough of them, perhaps you'll be lucky enough to have someone with four degrees on the wall behind her tell you this:

> *"You're unqualified to do anything we do around here. Do you even know what we do? Don't answer me, tell Sally at the front desk on your way out. Thank you."**

> ** True story*

I think it's incredibly difficult to determine if you are unqualified for a job based on the title and the *perceived* level of difficulty in doing that job. So you'll need to develop your own method for determining what jobs are difficult and what the expectations might be. Don't let job posters tell you that. Don't let anyone tell you what is difficult – they don't know you. I'm not trying to tell you that the following table is full of hard or easy jobs. It is just my list and assessment of the difficulty and level of expectations. You can take my information and use it to form your own but you shouldn't listen to what I say… Why? …Because I don't have nice tits.

The following thought process is going to sound abnormal to you, not like everything before which is clearly Pulitzer worthy, but rest assured that this abnormality is completely normal to me:

> *"There is no correlation between how difficult a job sounds and what the expectations are in doing that job well."*

– Brad Myers

There it is. To help you think along this brilliant line of thinking, I've put together a couple of tables. The first table lists some jobs that are commonly thought of as difficult, typically based on name alone. The first column is the job title, the next column displays my perceived difficulty in doing that job, and the third column explains the expectations on doing that job well. The second table covers jobs that are commonly (and sometimes incorrectly) thought of as easier. In no particular order, here is the first table:

Table 1: "Difficult" Jobs

Job	Difficulty	Level of Expectations
Commercial Airline Pilot	Zero. You've heard the term, "These things fly by themselves nowadays." A pilot said that. They just hit a button to turn on the autopilot and play Angry Birds and drink martinis in the cockpit. All those buttons, levers, and switches? For show – so they can charge more.	The level of expectations of a pilot performing well is very high for passengers because we all want to get to Las Vegas alive for the hookers and blow. However, the expectations are incredibly low from the employers' perspective because, "These things fly by themselves nowadays."

Job	Difficulty	Level of Expectations
Test Pilot	Probably high since you might be flying prototypical aircraft where they haven't installed the autopilot yet.	None, but with huge upside. Everyone expects the cartoon-like airplane they glued together to crash anyway. You're supposed to die so the expectations are minimal. But you do a loop-de-loop and fly that thing upside down and you're a hero!
Architect	Seems difficult, but there is a lot of drawing and coloring involved, so this is a job a five year old does today, so it's easy.	High. This job is high profile because everyone sees buildings and if they aren't sound they fall on people.
Landscaper	Sounds easy, but it's not.	Customers have high expectations making this difficult. You can't butcher their lawn or leave turds and weeds, that's bad form. You're also working with equipment and other workers that can, and sometimes want, to kill you.

Job Difficulty and Their Level of Expectations

Job	Difficulty	Level of Expectations
Air Traffic Controller	Pretty easy. You're looking at a video game panel of multiple airplanes in the sky immediately around you. Just don't run them into each other or land them on top of one another (or people), and you're good. Push reset as needed.	High/Low. You're really concealed away, literally in a tower, from the fact that there are people's lives at stake based on what you do at your video game control panel. So the expectations put on you by others (employer, passengers) are very high. But personally, you have little to worry about, you're not in danger and you get to put in another quarter and play again tomorrow.
Brain Surgeon	Assumingly difficult only because it sounds like it.	High expectations of doing the job correctly, brains are important.
Rocket Scientist	Probably difficult, but not as difficult as people make it out to be.	Everyone makes this reference when they think something or someone is really complicated or smart. So I put it on the list but I'm not sure the expectations are very high. Can you make a rocket go from here to there and then blow up? Hired!

Job	Difficulty	Level of Expectations
Alaskan Crab Fishing	None. It's fishing…And it's for crab! You float around on the sea setting traps for stupid sea creatures. Then drink some beers, come back later and pull up the traps. From shore, you can just drink beer and walk through the eel grass in shallow salt water until you kick one – then bend over and pick it up.	Huge expectations that you stay on the boat and alive. I guess there is a show on television about how dangerous this is. The real danger is being at sea, with other men, and all you have are tiny biceps and what the captain called a "sea-worthy-ass." Whatever that means. AHOY!
Cardiologist	Difficult – there's a rib cage and lungs and other stuff connected that needs to be paid attention to. The brain surgeon really just needs to get through a skull and – poof – there's your brain.	I'm sure it's hard to open a chest and work on a heart, but I'm not sure the expectations are really that high on you. Most people hear that someone had heart surgery and are more surprised that they lived through it than anything. So I think the expectations are low, but the reward for success is high. Winning!

The following table covers jobs that may not be considered difficult, based on false perceptions, and may or may not come with lower expectations. These jobs might be more suited to your needs. To finish up this chapter, here is a short list of some sample jobs you might be good at:

Table 2: "Easy" Jobs

Job	Difficulty	Level of Expectations
Men's room attendant	Not terribly difficult in skill, but you have to stand in a room where men poop and pee. And you have to hand them towels and smile in an ass-gas filled room. Nasty!	Low. You know penises. You can work a faucet and hand a dude a towel, but not much is expected of you – other than to leave me the hell alone. If you can refrain from doing the following, you can get hired: 💩 Staring 💩 Gawking 💩 Gazing 💩 Giving handies (actually might be a requirement for securing the job) 💩 Making fart noises with your mouth 💩 Complimenting penises

Job	Difficulty	Level of Expectations
Weight Guesser at a Carnival	This is a very difficult job because you're constantly calling someone fat. And fat people get mean when you call them fat. I know, because I'm mean all the time. And sad.	Pretty low. Pick a number; larger numbers for fat people. Only feelings get hurt. You're expected to hand out useless stuffed animals and plastic novelty glasses. Occasional risk of being beaten up by angry boyfriends.
Circus Bear	Incredibly difficult depending on the type of bear you are portraying: Brown, Polar, bottom, Black, Grizzly. But circus bears are just you in a bear suit.	If you're wearing a bear suit in a circus show and have to dance in a tutu and/or ride a unicycle, you don't want to fall and hurt yourself, but that's exactly what the crowd wants, so their expectations on your performance is huge. And if any of you suggest that those are real bears, you're on crack – real bears eat people that go to circuses.

Job	Difficulty	Level of Expectations
Rodeo Clown	Easy. Wait, no, difficult. Well, it can be difficult if you're stupid, slow, or both.	Make a bull mad at you, run around and not get gored. The customer expectations are high that you take a horn up your pooper and get tossed over the fence making this appear to be a difficult job. But it's on the easy list because you're wearing makeup and clown clothes.
Fast food preparation	Can be difficult for the same reasons as rodeo clown above. Also, people hate you and make fun of you behind your back, but you know it anyway.	Menus are sometimes extensive, but training is excellent and everything is done in an assembly line. It's like building cars except this is people food. Customers have high expectations but you're employer really just doesn't want you spitting on or diseasing the food.
Strip club DJ	Sweet!	I may have mentioned this earlier, but it has to be the best job EVAR! Difficult or not, the expectations are that you play the right music at the right time or the whole process breaks down and someone gets broke!

Job	Difficulty	Level of Expectations
Trebuchet operator	Sure, not a lot of call for this these days, but who cares, it's totally awesome! Make flaming rock hit people. Make dead cow fly over fence. Awesome!	Low. Everyone knows how inaccurate these things are. Just getting it loaded and launched is going to beat any expectations someone might have. Your employer and anyone watching is just gonna stand by and say, "*F-Yeah! I love America!*"

So don't let society tell you which jobs are difficult and which are easy… I just did that for you. You know what you're capable of and what you want to do, focus on what is going to make you happy, it's really the only thing you can control. Assess the jobs you want to apply for and make the determination if the difficulty level and/or the expectations that will be placed on you are something you're willing to accept.

Most jobs aren't going to be fun; you have to make them that way. The job where your personality is wanted is the best fit for you – that's why some of you don't work. But keep interviewing; you'll land the job you want some day. If you can find an easy job with low expectations on you to perform well, then apply for it quick because there's a good chance my resume is in that pile on the desk – and you do NOT want to go boner-to-boner with me in an interview.

Chapter 4:

OOA

One of the confusing things about technology jobs is the overuse of acronyms (OOA) to describe things. Employers and co-workers can say entire sentences in interviews that contain few, if any, actual words and it makes sense to them. People can come off sounding smart while making you feel like an idiot for not understanding Computer as a Second Language (CSL).

The OOA in technology is never going to change. It's an accepted, efficient way to communicate ideas and describe commonly used statements. In the world of "texting" it's a must-do or your sausage fingers would cramp trying to type "rolling on the floor laughing out loud" at that picture of the cat doing that funny thing…Have you seen that one? LMFAO!!!

For example, I once interviewed for a company that developed marketing software – they made software tools for marketing firms or something like that (I obviously didn't get that job). At one point I asked about their tools and how they were developed:

Unemployed Me: *"So, tell me about these marketing tools?"*

Smart interviewer dude: *"We use OOP, C#, C++ utilizing CAD and PCAD. We IM over XMPP, with*

LDAP for lookups, and we clear all issues in our Crossfire Unix Network Troubleshooter."

I drifted off while he spoke, but didn't understand until now why he didn't "acronym-ize" the name of that last tool, that's funny! Anyway, he sounded too smart for me to want to work there. I can quickly tell if I'm going to fit in at a work place. For example, in an interview, if I don't immediately feel like I'm going to be able to sift to the bottom and go unrecognized and underutilized for at least five years, I'll walk and look elsewhere. It's not that I'm unmotivated; it's just that everyone else seems to be so much <u>more</u> motivated than me. If I'm asked where I want to be in five years and, *"Tanning on a beach because I'm passed out drunk"* makes them smirk in disgust, I'll hike a cheek and fake like I'm farting and leave the interview.

In all of my interviews, I want at least one of us laughing at something, and I've never failed to accomplish that. Regardless of whether I'm laughing about something that's happening during the interview or the interviewer is laughing at my qualifications; we both have a good time. And sure, only one of us leaves those interviews with a job, but I like to think I make people happy.

Anyway, this particular interview seemed a little heaped in "work," with all those "techy" words, so I made up my mind that if I could get past the following conversation and receive a callback, then I'd consider working there.

Smart Interviewer Dude: *"So, Jib, what are your passions?"*

Unemployed Me: *"Mostly websites."*

Smart Interviewer Dude: *"Oh, do you build or design them?"*

Unemployed Me: *"No, I click on them, buy things from them, and generally do stuff to myself while looking at them."*

Smart Interviewer Dude: *"Um, what?"*

Unemployed Me: *"Anyway, given my blistering thirty words-per-minute typing skills, and Internet porn site database, tripled with my commitment to excellence; how can I help your team be more successful?"*

Smart Interviewer Dude: *"Are you serious? I have other candidates that I need to interview today, is this really what you want to say to me?"*

Unemployed Me: *"Whoa, what did you think I said?"*

Smart Interviewer Dude: *"Sir, you mentioned "Internet porn" in a job interview. We don't tolerate that around here."*

Backpedaling Me: *"Internet porn? NO, no, I'm sorry, I meant Internet CORN, the yellow vegetable; that's completely different than Internet porn... I love the maize! So I keep a database of different corn sites for easy viewing. Why? Do you know of some sites I might want to see? Corn or porn? You know, for research?"*

If he's laughing, then this might be the place for me. If he's dialing 9-1-1, it's not. See, my lot in life is to work for a company where I become like those extra nuts and bolts at the bottom of a tool box. I've wiggled to the bottom underneath larger, more valuable nuts and bolts, but I'm not worth throwing away because I don't take up much space and you just never know when you'll need a cheaper fastener for a crappy job you don't want to waste your good bolts on.

I set the tone right up front in the interview. Matter of fact, the tone is probably already set based on stuff the interviewer has read on my resume prior to the interview. Essentially, it's only fair if the interviewer knows what s/he's getting into. Sure, it limits my opportunities for better jobs because they typically want good workers for those jobs, but if it isn't clear yet: I'm not really interested in working.

Acronyms are used incessantly in technology offices. Investigate what your prospective companies do and what terminology they might use – create your own acronyms to repeat during the interview. You might look smart explaining what they mean, and that's BP for you! (BP=Bonus Points. See, it's pretty easy and incredibly brilliant.)

Learn your acronyms; put a lot of them on your resume, even if you don't know what they are. When asked during the interview about them, just say,

"It's hard to explain, I have something I can forward you when I get home."

The OOA in the technology industry really doesn't bother me because I'm so used to it in my regular life. IMO, from my POV, my life is much better when I get to eat BLT's, take regular BMs, and drive my MG and crank a CD on my way to the YMCA. That may be TMI for you, but here's an FAQ: WTF? I'm just trying to share my standard MO to help you. Oh, and BTW, for new people to the technology industry, you should brush up on your technology acronyms ASAP and insert some in your resume, and start practicing them at home. You'll sound smarter.

Chapter 5:

Pretty People

There is something far worse than the OOA, and that is the blatant objectification of pretty people. Pretty people are used to attract new technology talent by placing them in television commercials, in brochures, and even sending them to recruitment events. Certainly, pretty people are used on company web sites which lead you to believe those people actually work there. It's something we really can't do anything about other than be aware of it. It's a horrible topic and I'm embarrassed to even point it out, but there is a huge lack of attractive people in the technology industry. There, I said it.

Certainly there are exceptions, but this is my single biggest complaint about the technology industry. Now I'm not a pretty person or even a sensitive one, but I do take a few necessary precautions to make sure I don't come to work looking like I'm losing the battle of ugly:

1. I shower at least once a week, whether I need it or not.
2. I trim all visible hair that grows above my collar. This includes head, face, nose, and ear hair, including the eyebrows ("eyebrows" is plural, meaning there should be two or more, but never just one).
3. I do not wear pants that have been trapped in my bicycle chain.

4. I do not wear shirts that have food stains that I can't provide an explanation for.
5. I don't wear makeup, but if I did I'd follow these rules:
    a. Always use less than a clown.
    b. Use the same color on each eye.
    c. Lipstick goes on the lip part; there is a definitive line that separates your lip from the rest of your face, stop there.
    d. Moles are already black, using makeup to make them darker makes people want to pluck them off or pop them and that's not safe.
    e. Putting putty in cracks in dry wall never looks like the original. Makeup in your wrinkles draws attention to them and makes other people stare. Your wrinkles are beautiful experiences coming out of your face.
    f. Fake eyelashes are fine because they are longer and thicker resulting in better safety protection from things falling from above. I condone. However, don't take them off in front of me- creepy.
    g. Makeup is an enhancement to, not a replacement for, your face. Less is more.

It's not a very high bar to get over, is it? Yet we still see many folks fighting some or many of these issues every day. Again, I realize I'm not handsome and I understand how insensitive and inappropriate this topic is. But here's the connection: the more you are around a certain type of people, the more that type of people become your "norm." You raise or lower your standards based on your exposure to certain types of people. If you've been married for several years, you and your partner will start to dress, and in some cases, even look alike.

We tend to lower the bar based on our surroundings, influenced by our state of mind. For example, if you've ever gotten drunk in a bar you know that the more alcohol you drink, the prettier the people seem to be. Your personal taste in "what's pretty" is influenced by your state of mind; in this case, drunk. Well, at work it's the same thing only it takes a bit longer because for the most part you aren't supposed to drink at work. So at work it's mostly your surroundings that influence what you perceive as pretty or not so pretty.

For example, Helga in Accounting was barely a "1" two years ago. It's important to note that she got to "1" ONLY because she has tits…not nice tits, she just actually has them. Now it's been two years and given the hiring practices, the current talent pool, and your exposure to constant ugly, Helga's a "5" because your standards have succumbed to the environment.

So when you're interviewing for a job, keep in mind that how attractive the people are isn't really important lie because you'll adapt your taste to suit your surroundings. In a matter of weeks, everyone will be prettier under those terms and you'll feel like settling. I should point out that it is never acceptable to judge people by their appearance lying. It's ok to judge people, just be sure to throw in another parameter like this;

> "She's ugly, but she also has big feet, I don't like her because of her feet."
>
> "He's ugly, but he also has small feet, I don't like him because he has a small penis, I mean feet, he has small feet."

But saying you don't like someone only because they are ugly is just rude and mean. Interview with an open mind and don't pay any attention to appearances because it won't matter in the long run~~lying~~. If you're lucky enough to work where there are a lot of pretty people then kudos to you, you don't need my help. There is a saying about beauty only being skin deep, but that was said by an ugly person with really thick skin – gross! I forgot what I was talking about but I'm not hungry any more…

Oh yeah, pretty people: we need more of them. When researching prospective employers and going on interviews, be aware that what you see in print or televised advertisements aren't necessarily a true representation. I know; it was hard for me to hear that when I first learned it. Don't believe what you see. If a company web site shows pretty people working a forklift – it's a lie. If the television commercial shows an attractive woman helping a new hire get situated in his new cubicle – also a lie. Lower your expectations in all interviews and there's a better chance you'll be pleasantly surprised rather than sorely disappointed.

Chapter 6:

Answering Email

The exchange of ideas, text, pictures, and pornography is what the Internet is all about. The biggest impact the Internet has had on society is in the way we connect and communicate with one another. Whether you are selling something on eBay and connecting with potential buyers, or you are purchasing a self-promoting pig's book, *"Paid to Poop"* from Amazon.com, you are communicating with other people over the Internet. For many people, electronic communication has taken over as their primary means of keeping in touch with family and friends. The telephone still allows you nearly instant communication, but how often do you really need to hear your sibling's raspy voice filtered through phlegm and false teeth? The Internet has changed the way we connect with each other, and in the workplace it's important to stay "in the know" on current communication protocol.

In this chapter, you'll learn how email offers people another way to communicate in spite of their verbal challenges. You'll also be exposed to some possible racial profiling, but you'll learn how and when to respond to work email based on who your audience is. This chapter is complete with sample emails and texting jargon, some insensitivity, and a couple of swear words. Let's get started with email and how it helps people communicate.

Email has closed the distance between family and friends and provides for efficient means of communication between coworkers. My favorite thing about email is that it allows people to transcend their own speaking deficiencies. You no longer have to listen to a Stutterer, Yeller, or Mushmouth talker because their actual speech is never heard in email. However, you can still "hear" their personal voice while reading their email so you never lose the reason you hated talking to them in the first place. Email can be tricky, though, as it requires you to know your audience.

The people you speak with on a daily basis have different voices and this might affect you in different ways. Some people might be soft talkers and make you feel comfortable, while others may be aggressive and brash and make you feel mean. If everyone you speak with on a daily basis makes you feel comfortable, you probably work in or spend a large amount of time in a massage parlor, or luxurious spa. The reality is, at work, you probably speak to more annoying people than you do less-annoying people. Email can help everyone communicate on a less-annoying plane. There are many different face to face speaking styles, and following are just a few examples of how email impacts our communication.

Close Talkers – If your listeners seem to slowly tip backwards or draw their neck away from you when you're telling another lame story, you're probably a Close Talker. Perhaps your depth perception is out of whack or you like the smell of your own breath bounced off someone else's face. Doesn't matter, you should really carry mints (spear or pepper) and toss one in your cake hole before communicating with other people face on face.

Obviously, email helps you get your point across without spitting on people or invading their circle of private space. Close talkers tend to receive twice as much email as they send because everyone is uncomfortable talking with them. However, Close Talkers can solve their communication problem in two ways; email or mints. Personally, I don't mind talking to a Close Talker if her breath smells like spearmint and/or she has nice breasts.

English as Second Language (ESL) Talkers – If English is your second, third, or worst language you face more challenges than most. If you ask questions in meetings and the moderator usually asks, *"I'm sorry, I couldn't hear your question-- could you repeat it?"* That moderator is lying and the real issue is your accent. It is entirely possible that your accent is so heavily laden with mumbo-jumbo that all your listeners hear are a bunch of clicks and whistles when you speak. Email allows you to enter your questions in a readable format that your listener cannot lie about misinterpreting. Unless you sneakily encode .wav files of clicks and whistles in the email and then that's just really funny.

Lisp Talkers – If you don't think of yourself as a particularly funny person but people giggle at what you have to say, you're probably a Lisp Talker. The slaughtering of many words by putting an extra "s" or "sh" in them goes away in the typewritten world of email. I had a speech impediment until I was in the third grade. I slurred the letter "s" and "sh" more often back then than I look at porn on the Internet now. Obscure reference? Maybe, but you don't realize how bad the impediment was nor how much sshhhexy porn I actually view. Again, just like an ESL Talker can use .wav files, if you purposely type an extra "s" or "sh" in your email words then that's just freaking funny! Email helps you get your point across without having to be giggled at.

Mushmouth Talkers – If you sound like Mushmouth from *"The Fat Albert Show"* then your tongue is probably too big for your mouth. Don't know Mushmouth? YouTube it.

Maybe your hat is pulled down past your eyes and impairs your speech. Mushmouth was funny on Saturday morning cartoons, but he'd be a nightmare to work with and just another dude needing some kind of surgery to make him "right." So if you typically mumble like you have a mouth full of marbles when you speak, nobody will care if you email them. Email allows you to set a filter to stop adding extra "b's" to everything you type. However, if you can wear a stocking cap pulled over your eyes, speak with mostly "b's" and still have people understand you, you should be running your own company.

Soft Talkers – Soft Talkers often create Close Talkers because you can't hear the words coming out of a Soft Talkers mouth unless you lean in close. Is it worth appearing creepy to hear what a Soft Talker is saying? Usually not because they lack the confidence in what they are saying and if they don't care, why should you? If I have to work at listening to someone, I've already lost interest and started thinking about an exit strategy. Sometimes, I'll just fart knowing a Soft Talker isn't going to say anything. Then I'll just point at them and back away slowly. But my favorite retaliation is to throw the soft talk routine right back at them with a whispered classic; *"Sphincter-says-what?"*

Stutterers – Everyone knows a stutterer. Well, I don't, but most people probably know a stutterer. Ok, that's not necessarily true either. How about this; most people know what stuttering is…? Well, when a Stutterer speaks, s/he sounds like records skipping … You know when the needle hits something in the groove or a scratch and it… "record"? "needle"?… Oh yeah, I'm really old – stuttering is when you have difficulty saying words without repeating the initial syllable multiple times. Actually, it's not always just the initial syllable; dictionary.com defines stuttering as:

"To speak in such a way that the rhythm is interrupted by repetitions, blocks or spasms, or prolongations of sounds or

syllables, sometimes accompanied by contortions of the face and body."

OMG, when you stop laughing at that definition, read on without me because I'm still laughing! Sorry, it just paints a fantastic picture.

Anyway, if you stutter, you might say things like this:

"Yyyyyour ass is fat."

If you begin most sentences with too many syllables, then email is the perfect tool to help you sound less stupid. Because, in email, "your" isn't eight letters long and has only one "y." Now I know stuttering can be a genetically determined trait and/or a hiccup in the developmental stage of life, so it's not something to laugh about – out loud,… and to other Stutterers – but it's hilarious amongst your regular-speaking friends. Bottom line; stuttering isn't cool, unless you're singing George Thorogood's *"Bad to the Bone."* Email helps stutterers be more efficient and clear in their communications, thus eliminating that awkward feeling for speaker and listener.

Yellers – Your voice sounds normal to you. You think the crinkled face and squinted eye of your listener is a form of intense concentration and excellent listening skills. However, that's not the case, your voice is so loud you're actually breaking tiny membranes in their ear drums and their face twists in reaction to pain. They are just too kind to tell you to use your camping voice and don't want to insert ear plugs every time you want to talk about your dumb mother-in-law. Email helps you sound like a normal person, unless you use ALL CAPS when you email, then you're annoying and craving attention. Get a job helping the deaf – they need people to help and you need to be someplace you're wanted.

I am sure there are other categories of communicators that I haven't covered above but I just listed the more common ones that I have worked with. If you know more, perhaps there is another category just for you called, "Know it All." Anyway, email provides a way for people with various verbal communication "challenges" to become more effective communicators.

There is another area of importance to consider when using email to communicate with fellow office workers; the "Who, When, What" method of replying.

"Who, When, What" is an approach to replying to email that will help you focus on your target audience and allow you to respond in a way that will look favorably on you. It's about making yourself look busy, appear smarter or less stupid than you are, and create an aura of importance around you. I'm not real sure about that aura thing; I really just needed a third item and "aura of importance" sounded cool and made me look smarter. See that? I'm even doing it right now!

Here is a summary of these three components:

1. **Who** – This is an assessment of the person or persons you should or should not include when responding.
2. **When** – Determines when you should respond.
3. **What** – This is the content of your message and what you should consider when you do create your response.

It sounds complicated, but you might be doing this already and just don't realize it. If you aren't already doing this then applying it will become second nature to you after just a few days of trying this approach.

The following sections describe a few of the "Who's" in the workforce, and then explains the "When" and "What" to respond. Finally, I present an example to help drive home the concept. As with everything I do, which is half-assed, there are probably other "Who's" that I've left out. Review the following "Who's" and apply the concept to your email replies today. However, just like with cocaine and masturbation, everything in moderation, so salt this concept in with your usual method of replying so nobody becomes suspicious of your new found smarts and "busy-ness."

<u>Who</u>: <u>The Go-Getter</u>

This type of person dominates meeting conversations, always has something to say about anything, and receives managerial "acceptance nods" when s/he speaks out. They wall paper their office with awards of achievement and/or certifications of completion for training seminars. They use words like "synergy" and "paradigm," and include statements like "moving forward" and "cross functional," in normal conversation. They often carry a coffee mug, work later than some, and smile less than most. When the Go-Getter sits on a toilet, he's not thinking about getting paid to poop, he's thinking things like;

> *"Geez this is a waste of time, I should just wear adult diapers and save myself the trouble."*

When to reply: Always reply after the first or second response has already come in. Wait until someone else has responded and then you come in with an intelligent statement or question with respect to something that was in any of the original emails. Don't ask what's already been answered, you'll blow your cover. Pick out something you think others might think is important to know. You don't have to actually want to know the answer but it can help with credibility.

What to reply: The Go-Getter is not your enemy as you might expect. This person has enough people looking up to him or her, so don't be another drone – but don't disrespect either. They have enough clout with management that any negative words can be negative for you. This person helps keep your company "moving forward" – carrying you along. Nurture this person. Try using buzz words and/or phrases that attract attention. Remember, there are no "problems" only "challenges." Also try using words like; champion, best practice, proactive, and facilitate. For example;

> *"I see some challenges here that I'd like to champion an initiative to help form a best practice to facilitate necessary changes to prevent this from happening moving forward."*

A statement like that gets management panties wet but is completely non-committal. You've actually agreed to do nothing other than root for the start of some process others should create. High-five! You've also used keywords, like champion and facilitate, which pop out during performance reviews like hemorrhoids on a manager's ass. You're tickling the sphincter of the promotion repository with stuff like this and I think something's about to slide your way. Lots of references to "assholes" in this section about Go-Getter's and Management – weird, huh?

Example: A message from a customer comes into a support alias that many team members are monitoring; including Larry, Alice, Brenda, and yourself. Here's a screenshot of that actual email thread. Remember, you have to start reading from the bottom up. Favorite part? Brenda's signature:

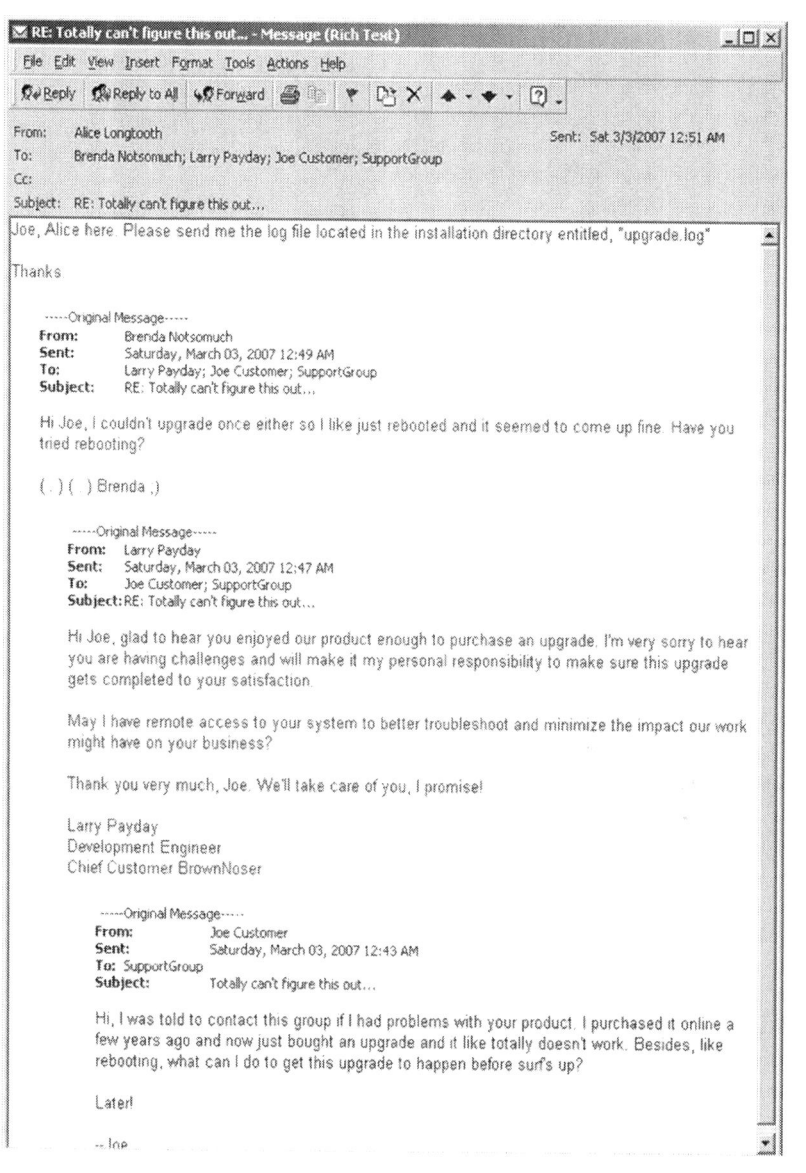

RE: Totally can't figure this out... - Message (Rich Text)

From: Alice Longtooth Sent: Sat 3/3/2007 12:51 AM
To: Brenda Notsomuch; Larry Payday; Joe Customer; SupportGroup
Cc:
Subject: RE: Totally can't figure this out...

Joe, Alice here. Please send me the log file located in the installation directory entitled, "upgrade.log"

Thanks

-----Original Message-----
From: Brenda Notsomuch
Sent: Saturday, March 03, 2007 12:49 AM
To: Larry Payday; Joe Customer; SupportGroup
Subject: RE: Totally can't figure this out...

Hi Joe, I couldn't upgrade once either so I like just rebooted and it seemed to come up fine. Have you tried rebooting?

(.) ( ) Brenda ;)

-----Original Message-----
From: Larry Payday
Sent: Saturday, March 03, 2007 12:47 AM
To: Joe Customer; SupportGroup
Subject: RE: Totally can't figure this out...

Hi Joe, glad to hear you enjoyed our product enough to purchase an upgrade. I'm very sorry to hear you are having challenges and will make it my personal responsibility to make sure this upgrade gets completed to your satisfaction.

May I have remote access to your system to better troubleshoot and minimize the impact our work might have on your business?

Thank you very much, Joe. We'll take care of you, I promise!

Larry Payday
Development Engineer
Chief Customer BrownNoser

-----Original Message-----
From: Joe Customer
Sent: Saturday, March 03, 2007 12:43 AM
To: SupportGroup
Subject: Totally can't figure this out...

Hi, I was told to contact this group if I had problems with your product. I purchased it online a few years ago and now just bought an upgrade and it like totally doesn't work. Besides, like rebooting, what can I do to get this upgrade to happen before surf's up?

Later!

-- Joe

- Larry responded to the customer first letting them know the team is working on it.
- Brenda threw in her one cent (that's all she has) by asking the customer to do something he already tried.
- Alice mentioned a specific log file that the customer should send for review.

You should now jump on the thread, remove the customer, and ask questions that haven't already been answered by anyone on the thread. Be generic in your response; ask questions your teammates will know the answer to because it empowers them. Here are three examples of responses to each person:

You to Larry only: *"Larry, do you know what version they are using and could that be an issue?"*

You to Alice only: *"Alice, good suggestion, are there other log files that might be handy for troubleshooting?"*

You to Brenda only: *"Brenda, WTF?"*

Who: The Asians

Depending on where you are, "Asian" can mean different things. For the purposes of this ridiculous book, "The Asians" refer to people of The Far East, The Indian Subcontinent, and Southeast Asia. So when I slip and say, "Indian," I mean a person of India decent, not the guy in those 1970's television commercials wearing a feathered head dress crying by the side of the road over tossed garbage.

Asians are always smarter than you – accept it. Even if you are Asian, you probably see another Asian in the room and think the same thing others do:

"I bet s/he's smarter."

Unless of course you work at an Indian casino, then this "smarter-than-you" concept may not apply but "drunker-than-you" probably does. Inappropriate, I know. This isn't about me needing sensitivity training (been there – failed that), it's about understanding that while you were eating pie as a fat, white American elementary school student, an Asian was figuring pi to the 69th decimal. While the slow, white American stuffed Dorito's in his face on the couch wasting his freedom, an Asian wrote code to manipulate rockets and space satellites to help create his. They're smarter and prettier. I'm just stating what we already know.

When to reply: Respond if directed at you and/or you know the answer. If you don't know the answer and you offer up some lame retarded response, you risk a verbal assault in broken English. It's simply too confusing to respond to an assault like this;

"You not know COM, you not know DOM tree – you better to stuck weeth what you know, which is be what you can, white dog."

I'm just making this stuff up trying to be funny – I can't stress enough the need for sensitivity training in matters like these. Keep an open mind or someone is going to open it for you.

What to reply: They were smarter in grade school and they are smarter in the work force. You can't compete and if you do, you might look like the person batting down the foreigner. Oh, and never use the type of language I'm using now, it's bad form and mostly unacceptable unless you're in a fight – and never fight them – they know Kung-Fu or Tae Bo. Just plug your nose and keep walking by their office and never go in the kitchen when they're using the microwave. Once again, sensitivity training is an excellent start to opening your mind to diversity.

Example: Bonjaba sends an email to your team asking if he can modify a COM object that accesses the kernel to allow slip streaming of the JDBC driver to access SQL or MSDE based on SMTP over TCP/IP but invoked by CSST and triggered when eating a PB&J or while driving a BMW.

> 💩 It's best to let the smart people handle this. Even if you know the answer to the horrible example above, you won't gain any credibility due to the fact that they are smarter than you. However, there is a good chance your penis is bigger.

Who: The Intern

This person is also smarter than you because she has two years of community college where she learned introduction to business by blowing teachers for grades and beer money. Interns are always treated with disrespect unless they have – Anyone? Anyone? – nice tits. So if you don't have nice tits, or you're a dude and someone once said you had nice tits, you'll always be disrespected as an Intern.

However, the Intern is also typically very motivated and will participate in all email conversations. Interns are cute with their willingness to help, and typically have high energy and youthful arrogance. I suppose it's better to encourage them and not squash their dreams for the sake of your own entertainment. But it's really fun to poop in their desk drawer and see if they'll say something or just clean it up themselves – either way you get to laugh, and probably go to jail.

When to reply: Later. It's always best to wait to reply to anything an Intern says unless they've said something like;

> "*I'm planning to blow this place up!*" or "*I've got two hand guns, failed mid-terms, and a hankerin' for some bloodshed!*"

At that point it's best to leave the office. Never reply to an intern in the first hour of receiving any message. Whatever the Intern has typed is never important, and if you reply too soon then you're giving them the impression that it was important. See what I mean? Even if what they say is important_it's not_, you can't reply too soon or they'll know it's important_it's not_ and that just builds their confidence and they'll keep yappin'. So just reply later or not at all.

What to reply: The more confusing the better. Make reference to something you've never told them or be completely obscure in your explanation. Otherwise, you risk the chance of looking really stupid if they do know, thus reaffirming their arrogance and that A+ they got in sociology. Interns are arrogant and outspoken and probably know your job better than you. I hate interns, unless… Anyone? Anyone? Same answer as before. BOO-YA!

Example: Betsy, your HR representative (oops, sorry, another acronym – HR stands for Human Resources: A business department where you are a replaceable resource, not a person) has sent an email to you and cc'd your intern requesting some payroll information. The Intern has responded first to both of you offering up the correct information. You should wait one hour, minimum, then reply as if you didn't see the response:

> **You to The Intern only:** *"Hey Intern, remember that website I told you to look at and fill in your information for HR so they can process your paycheck? Did you ever do that? Seems HR is looking for answers."*

When the Intern responds stating they don't recall the conversation with you (notice there is no way to prove a verbal conversation took place as there is with written email), you simply lie again... And don't act surprised about all this lying, you know you've done it, liar;

> **You to The Intern only:** *"I guess that might have been one of my OTHER interns I told. Doesn't matter, I just spoke with someone else in HR and they've since removed that site. I see you've responded with the information needed. I'll send things in email from now on."*

<u>Who</u>: <u>The Slacker</u>

The Slacker takes extra-long to complete anything, wastes meeting time with pointless questions, keeps cold cuts in his office drawer, and rifles through other people's mail in the mailroom. We've all done these same things but the biggest difference between you and the Slacker is that for him, it's normal behavior.

The Slacker doesn't think he's slacking, he's just living. Any good Ninja will tell you that this kind of reckless abandon is the most dangerous. Well, stupid Ninja's might tell you that, real Ninja's don't say much at all. But if you know stupid Ninja's it doesn't matter because the fact you know <u>any</u> Ninja's makes you really cool! Ninja's KICK ASS! Anyway, keep your eye on the Slacker, but don't befriend him – you've got Ninja friends, keep them, you don't need Slacker friends.

Slacker friends just drag you down like when a hot stripper tells you you're hot and that you'd make a "smokin'" male dancer. But a week later you find yourself on a stage barely clothed and mostly embarrassed and twenty-five hot chicks laughing at your show and junk. F'ing slackers. What was I talking about?

When to reply: Doesn't matter when you reply, he doesn't care about the job so you'll just confuse him.

What to reply: The Slacker is not your enemy as long as you keep your communication short and do not confide in him or her. This is more difficult than it sounds because losers attract losers so the Slacker will associate well with what you are trying to accomplish. You may need to feign interest in a tough project and solicit his/her help – that'll disperse 'em.

Example: Email from Slow Bobby;

"What does the computer want when it asks for my "Password"? And does anyone have a Sharpie I can use for a little while?"

See, there are some stupid questions, and stupid people, and a question like this from a Slacker should scare you. A Sharpie in the hands of a Slacker can be bad news and nothing good can come from it. Everybody complains about Slow Bobby, but nobody tells him about it because they're scared. Unless he comes to work with a drawn on Hitler mustache and marches around with stiff arms and legs, you have to tolerate him. So your best response in this situation is to keep it short. You don't want to make a friend and you don't want to make an enemy. Something that empathizes and encourages is your best route. A good response to the example above might be:

You: *"Shoot, I don't remember. And I'm also looking for a Sharpie, I love 'em!"*

So there you have just a few examples of the varying personalities you might work with. Sure, there are many more personalities like the "Always Angry Guy," and the "Always Busy Guy." And there's also my favorite; "Hot Happy Hottie." I chose not to write about them because; I hate the Always Angry Guy, the Always Busy Guy is a liar, and the Hot Happy Hottie just makes me do things in the bathroom that I probably shouldn't be.

💩💩💩

I've covered a lot in this chapter; from the different types of face-to-face communicators you must tolerate every day, to the different personalities that you probably share one or two within yourself – you know who you are, both or all of you inside there (multiple personalities are hard to make fun of). I've provided examples of ways you can use email to avoid work and save time for more of what you want to do. I've given real world examples to help drive the concepts home and even slandered a couple of people and/or races. It's been a full day for me.

I've offensively and ineffectively shown how email is one tool that helped change communication between family, friends, and coworkers. There are many different personalities in the work force and finding the best way to communicate with them will help you be more accepted – certainly don't use my examples to reach that end. In addition to email and verbal communication there is a popular tool that is changing how teenagers cheat on tests, make hook ups, or tell each other they're pretty; texting.

Chapter 7:

Texting

If you've never used your cell phone for anything other than calling the pizza guy for your dinner and a dime bag, then you haven't unlocked your world to text messaging. I thought email was text messaging but "texting" is the term used for instantaneous text message delivery, typically from one teenager's cell phone to another. So if you haven't texted before then...

"*This texting stuff might make u feel like a n00b[1]. But WTF[2], with texting ur part of the L337[3] and can b the BMOC[4] if ur good at it...Or possibly have your HHIS[5] if ur a tool – either way, I'm ROTFL[6]!*"

Where email allows you to express your ideas and elaborate on topics more specifically, texting provides a new vernacular for teenagers and adults everywhere. For the older generation, it's really just a tool for your teenager to flirt and/or make plans for having sex – you know it's going to happen, let it go. Or perhaps older men use it for telling their partner, "Sorry for the "DITA" slip last night" (you'll have to look that one up yourself). Texting is like version 2.0 to my generations' equivalent of having your friend deliver "verbal mail":

"*Tell your friend that my friend thinks she's cute.*"

However, texting is easier, quicker, and more convenient than email, but it is more expensive. Texting how you feel is still less humiliating than having your friend spill your guts for you. Sometimes your friend will laugh at you with the cute girl and then those two will be sharing laughs and orgasms at your expense. Some friends and cute girls are mean.

Texting is prevalent and not going away. It's become an interruptive part of any physical conversation even when it's not a part of that conversation. For example, you can be speaking with a person when they receive a text and that text message will become the new focus of all communication. That text just became more important than whatever the two of you were discussing – even if you were discussing porn. Inconceivable!

You can see texting everywhere you look; at ball games, in moving vehicles, in the streets and in offices across the globe. I was pretty frustrated with the texting phenomenon because it just seemed so rude to me. I could see several people at any given time with their heads down, eyes focused on a tiny screen and not paying any attention to their surroundings. I noticed that people walking and texting seldom knew who was near them. It didn't matter to them; if for an arbitrary example, someone was hiding in the woods watching them. It's really scary, so I had an idea…

One day, I didn't have any interviews lined up and was pissed at *The Price is Right*, because some jack-wagon bid $510 when he just heard two bids of $501 and $525! I hate some people. Anyway, I grabbed my notebook and my second favorite set of pens and walked around my neighborhood, somewhat concealed from view, and took notes on where I saw teenage girls texting and otherwise not paying attention to their surroundings. Here were the places I checked out and saw several texting teenagers. And remember that it's not creepy if it's for research:

- Shopping malls
- On the bus
- In high schools
- At cheerleading and gymnastics events
- During youth girls equestrian shows
- Junior and Senior High School volleyball tournaments
- Behind bridal shops
- Planned Parenthood parking lot
- Dance parties
- In second floor bedrooms around my neighborhood
- Purdy Correctional Facility

As you can see, I probably need to be arrested, but notice that there is a lot of texting going on in this neighborhood – and this only covers one demographic: hot teenage girls. You could choose a different demographic and your research may yield different results, but I wouldn't care…because I'm covering hot teenage girls.

I'm still trying to figure texting out. Not what it is, but why I would need it. I don't have a smart phone, but I do rely heavily on email for near instant communication. If I need instant feedback I can use my phone to actually call people. I understand the less intrusive feature of texting (assuming sounds are turned off) versus receiving a phone call, but in either case – it's interrupting whatever is going on over there.

I currently do not text, nor do I stalk teenage girls; hot or otherwise. I suppose I will someday, in order to keep in touch with the youth of today (yes, I'm referring to both texting and stalking). But until then, my feelings are this: the physical conversation I am having with you – face to face – is the most important conversation to me. I feel it's important to respect one another and honor the beauty of being able to converse with each other in real time and physically connected through sight, sound, and touch.

However, I am a dying breed; for every person I know (and granted, I'm not very popular) texts and believes in it. Whenever we are having conversations and their phone rings, vibrates, or plays Iron Maiden's *"Number of the Beast,"* the opportunity of that text or call being more important than what we are talking about is too hard for weak people to ignore. Great, I just called the very few friends I do have, "weak." Ohhhh, that's why I'm not very popular – full circle people, full circle.

My days of being a "texting-hater" are numbered. My sons will soon be teenagers and have teenage girlfriends, and stalking them will be much easier if I learn to text and the slang that goes along with it. But I will always contend: stop texting and start paying attention to what's going on around you. You might just see some idiot texting and walking into a pole or stepping in front of a moving bus. And who doesn't want to see that? ... Liar, I know you YouTubed it.

---

1. **n00b** = slang text term for the slang term "newbie" or someone new to something—like you are new to texting slang, you silly idiot… I mean "SI."
2. **WTF** = What The Fuck?
3. **L337** = "leet" or elite
4. **BMOC** = Big Man On Campus – old slang used by old writers who have no idea what a text message is other than text and a message, which used to mean hand written phone numbers on liquor soaked cocktail napkins.
5. **HHIS** = Head Hanging In Shame – rarely used by anyone I may have made this one up…You can't tell.
6. **ROTFL** = Rolling On The Floor Laughing

Chapter 8:

The Potty Protocol

The word "protocol" is a noun and defines a set of rules of appropriate behavior or customs and regulations dealing with precedence and etiquette. For my purposes, it's a word that describes an acceptable way of doing things. Therefore, my Potty Protocol is a set of rules of appropriate behavior when entering a bathroom and deals with the choices you make with respect to bathroom etiquette. Most of this chapter will seem like common sense to some of the cleaner readers but will make no sense to the senseless jackass' that chat, crap, wipe, and leave without washing their hands.

The Potty Protocol isn't complicated but nobody really talks about it. In fact, most of the male readers are going to think; *"Duh,"* while reading this because they already know this stuff, yet still some other male readers are going to think; *"Duh,"* because that's how deep men think about most things. Duh.

Here is the Potty Protocol that everyone should understand and adhere to. I've listed them in approximate order of applicability, not necessarily in order of importance. A list is easier to remember and I think I've arranged these in the order you would use them. If you can only manage two things at a time, focus only on rules #3 and #4; give a bro his space, and wash your hands, respectively. Here are the four basic rules to follow:

1. Don't look anyone in the eyes.
2. Don't *start* any *conversations*.
3. Give a bro his space.
4. Wash your hands.

Potty Protocol should be a natural action for men when entering a bathroom. I'm not sure there is a protocol in the women's bathroom because they don't have urinals. Besides, women in bathrooms are just doing each other's hair and lifting their breasts and talking about guys, right? Most men will follow the protocol without a lot of thought about it, meaning they'll make the right choices just because they have a penis. Some men breach the protocol so bad, it can raise questions regarding their sexuality.

For instance, a Close Talker is going to crowd you by taking the urinal right next to you even though others are available. You could have some dude with garlic breath leaning over the short divider right in your face telling you about his latest project. He's breaking rules #1, #2, and #3 right from the start: he's looking you in the eyes, started a conversation, and he's crowding your space. By the way; I share a great way to handle situations like this later in this chapter, please read on.

The Potty Protocol should be followed in all office bathrooms occupied by your coworkers. When you're out clubbing on a Saturday night, all bets are off. At dance clubs, you're dealing with a whole new situation and if you followed the Potty Protocol there, you'd never get to pee. If you're out with your friends and the bathroom is packed, you're bound to have to look at someone or say something so just concentrate on not pissing on yourself or others. For those nights out on the town, you can practice the Potty Protocol, but don't expect it to be followed by anyone else. In the office, however, it's a must-be-followed protocol and anyone not following should be called out on it.

So here are the four rules explained in a little bit of detail followed by a few examples – with visual aids – to help demonstrate the different rules. Just read and absorb the information, if it isn't clear now, it will be later.

1. Don't look anyone in the eyes: Avoid direct eye contact.

There is at least one exception: you can look them in the eyes if you are looking into a mirror first. Some dudes adhere to this rule to the letter and will talk to you while looking at themselves in the mirror. That's ok, but a little creepy if you're the listener. It's as if they're talking to themselves and including you in the conversation – weird. For all other times you can look at your shoes, or admire the tile and grout lines on the wall behind the urinal.

If you are sitting in a stall and must peek through the cracks (you should never peek through the cracks – in or out!) to see who just came in the bathroom, be sure to look at them from the neck down – never make eye contact. If you've just walked into the bathroom, you should be able to tell if someone is in a stall by first glancing at the door. Closed and locked? Good indication someone's there. Glance at the floor for feet, but never look through the cracks! That's creepy and wrong and what are you expecting to see in there? Remember that old saying, *"Don't ask the question if you aren't going to like the answer?"* Well, the same thing applies here – because nothing good can come from you peeping on another dude while he's pooping, and you're not going to like what you see. Especially if crapping isn't the only thing he is doing in there!

2. Do not *start* any *conversations*: You should never be the first to speak, but it is ok for you to respond if someone else has broken this second rule.

I've italicized and underlined "start" and "conversations" because you shouldn't start any conversations unless absolutely necessary (you'll see exceptions in a later chapter where I address what can and cannot be said in a bathroom). However, if someone starts a conversation with you about a work project or asks you a question that requires you to answer, you are clear to breach rule number two and look them in the eyes – but it is never necessary in a bathroom. If you want to stop someone from talking to you at the urinal you can simply turn your entire body to face him thus giving him your attention and full directional spray, and ask, *"What's that about the project again?"*

Bathrooms are not the place for business talk. If someone wants to talk "shop" in the bathroom, just change the subject. What subject should you change it to? Chicks.

> **Douche bag**: *"Hey, you gonna get your results for the presentation done before Friday's project meeting?"*
>
> **You**: *"Do you like girls? 'Cause I like girls. I wonder if we're going to hire any hot interns this summer."*
>
> **Douche bag**: *"Funny. Seriously, we're sort of counting on your results to tie all this together, you know? It's lacking all synergy and we can't move forward without your vital contribution."*
>
> **You**: *"Really? You don't like girls? Who's hiring the interns this year, I hope ..."*
>
> **Douche bag**: *"YOU'RE PEEING ON ME!"*

To sum up the second rule: you can't *start* any *conversations,* but if you find yourself in one, you can refer to my chapter on "Bathroom Babble" to get yourself through. Until then, eyes down and mouth closed and you'll do just fine.

3. Give a "Bro" his space: Do not stand or sit next to anyone else in the bathroom if there are other options.

"Bro" is short for "Brother" and is a slang term men use to refer to other men when they feel a strong sense of friendship or camaraderie. It's replacing "Dude" just like "hot" replaced "cool" for when something is "awesome." Of course "awesome" is really popular now too, in fact, it's "hella" popular. What?

Anyway, this third rule is the foundation for the others and is really just natural behavior. It was hard to put this as the third rule in the list but it is by no means third in importance. I want to make sure that that's clear. It's actually the first in importance. If you follow only this rule, you'll eliminate many of the other hazards caused by not following the other rules.

You shouldn't want someone standing next to you at a urinal unless (anyone? anyone?) yep, again with the nice tits thing – but it must be a girl! It's also the same for the stalls; always take a stall that is at least one away from anyone else sitting in there. You don't want piss splatter on your Dockers from some other dude's pee stick and it's just creepy to be sitting next to another guy while crapping. If there are no open stalls or free urinals that are apart from other guys, just leave the bathroom, you might get a flush salute in thanks.

Rule #3 is the least discussed rule in this entire chapter but it's the most important. Follow this very important rule and the others will just make sense to you. If you have to dig deeper than this rule, then you are on thin ice and possibly about to commit an infraction.

4. Wash your hands: After using the urinal or the toilet or blowing your nose or performing some secondary butt-wiping, ALWAYS wash your hands.

Still, many people ramble through their lives spreading germs from their colon to other people in offices via door knobs, kitchen countertops, and community donuts. Actually, I have counted at my workplace and the ratio is exactly one out of three "men" do not wash their hands after peeing. But those numbers are a bit skewed because it's roughly the same people every day because we tend to be on the same schedule.

However, it's that guy who sometimes washes and sometimes does not wash that freaks me out. He finishes pooping, exits the stall and stands in front of the mirror adjusting his tie. For him, there must be some line that he has to cross each time in the bathroom that helps him decide whether he should leave clean or not.

> **Spotty Washer:** *"I scraped the pile on that last wipe—but it doesn't appear to have stuck. Who'll know?"*

Yeah, it's that gross in the men's bathroom. Or perhaps this sick bastard sat next to you one time and shook your hand in the hall...

> **Sick Bastard:** *"I think that was just bowl water, not pee. Did I have chocolate chips for lunch?"*

It's this type of reckless abandon from the uncontrolled germ spreader that has no real method to his madness that makes us all sick at work. If everyone followed a simple set of rules to help stop the spread of ass fungus, we'd all be healthier.

I had a real hard time not making this rule just as important as "Give a Bro his space." But I decided to list them in order of applicability rather than importance. So this is the last thing you do when you leave a bathroom. It's hard to believe so many people simply purge their colon, wipe their ass, and then leave the bathroom and proceed to touch the door handles, kitchen appliances, keyboards, and also shake hands with co-workers and customers without washing off the fecal matter.

In fact, here is a letter I wrote to a local Seattle Washinton radio contest which won first place! The prize was two tickets to a Seattle Mariners game. So, I guess I actually lost:

To:employees@<CompanyNameWitheld>.com
From:anonymous
Subject: Bathroom etiquette

A lot of us have nicknames. Some of you have nicknames you aren't aware of; StinkFinger Johnson, TurdHand Larry, and PissSmell Chuck. These are names you've earned from your lack of bathroom etiquette. I'm not sure what goes on in the women's bathroom, and I'm sure it's different than what I'm picturing in my head, but I touch the same door handles, keyboards, and lab equipment that you do. I'm tired of seeing you transfer your fecal matter from your ass to the door, to the kitchen, to the coffee machine, and to the utensils.

My four year old knows to wash his hands after using the toilet. I say that like the impact of a four year old knowing something you don't will make you understand, but I'm sure it's lost on you. How about this... Have you wiped your ass, gotten a little poo on your thumb and thought, "Wow, that's gross, I should wash that off when I'm done here?" Of course not, because that would make sense. You just march out of your stall and head straight for the door. Pigs.

Although I will forever use my FMPD to open doors (Fecal Matter Protection Device – a paper towel), I know my FMPD isn't as sanitary as my washed hands, but I'm not going to touch doors you've just wiped poo on. Wash your hands after using the bathroom… Even if you just fake it by turning the water on and acting like you're rinsing, at least I'd feel better if I ever high-fived your poop hand.

💩💩💩

For most guys, the Potty Protocol is common sense and they follow it more or less without really thinking about it. So what do you do about enforcing these rules in your work place poop room? This is really difficult because you have to bring it to the dumbass' attention that they are unkempt without getting yourself fired. On one hand you don't want to upset your coworkers or humiliate them, but on the other hand – well, they've got crap on that other hand and need to stop putting that crap on things we touch! Geez, I can't believe I have to actually tell people that!

Examples are excellent for explaining a tactful way to help someone realize that they might not look their best. Let's say someone at work has a piece of food stuck to their face. Most people will actually appreciate it if you were to say something like this to them:

> **You:** *"Hey, you've got a little schmutz on your cheek from eatin' a pizza pie."*

That person would probably brush away the morsel and thank you for saving them from further embarrassment. But if someone's zipper is undone you can't say anything because you don't want to get caught meat-gazing. The zipper is something you let them find out on their own the next time they go to the bathroom. So there are some things you can point out and some things you shouldn't. The fact that you have food on your face or that your zipper is down has no impact on me whatsoever, yet I may or may not tell you about it based on the personal level of the infraction. For example; if we are in a meeting together where you are giving a presentation, I won't point out that your fly is down because there is too much opportunity for a lot of people to see it. But if you and I are meeting my mother, I'll tell you to keep it in your pants because I'm tired of my friends hitting on my mom like that.

But when it comes to telling someone they should wash their hands after using the bathroom, it seems offensive and we don't do it in the workplace. Granted, the way I want to say it might be considered offensive:

Me: *"Hey, shitfinger, you just left the bathroom without washing and then picked up a bagel you didn't want. I, of course, came along after you and picked up the crap bagel, ate it, and licked my fingers clean. Oh, and I'm gonna be out sick next week because your germs in my colon are going to tear me a new asshole. Thanks."*

What can you do? You can take the passive aggressive approach (passive aggressive is just a fancy way of saying you're being a pussy about something but you are also mad). The pussy way is to just put up signs asking everyone to wash their hands after using the wash room. But if they don't use a sink to wash their hands after wiping their butt, they probably don't read signs in the bathroom either. Here are some other classic passive aggressive actions and even some good 'ol fully aggressive approaches that you can employ today to help get your message across:

- 💩 Make as much noise as possible when washing your own hands. Pound the soap dispenser. Smack the towel dispenser. Run the water real strong. These things might make you feel better but if a dude doesn't wash his hands after crapping, he's not going to understand your less than subtle hints. He's just going to think you're loopy and try to scurry out of the bathroom even faster.
- 💩 Write a note that states something about washing hands after using the bathroom. Then place that note on the offender's office floor, drop your trousers and shit on that note. Make sure you get it all on the paper, otherwise that's gross.
- 💩 Say things to yourself, or ask questions, while washing your hands when others are in the bathroom (this is a slight exception to rule #2 about not starting any conversations, but I feel these drastic times cause for drastic measures – break the rule):

  - ➤ *"Geez, I can't seem to get these fingers clean. Hey, you ever had problems washing your hands after taking a crap?"*
  - ➤ *"Wow, the water is really warm, almost makes me have to pee again ... But then I'd have to wash again. It's a vicious circle."*
  - ➤ *"Are you going to wash your hands when you're done?"*
  - ➤ *"I'm going to go ahead and leave the water running for you. Seems a shame to shut off that good clean water ... For washing your hands."*
  - ➤ *"This was weird the other day ... I washed my hands, reached for the door handle and got*

someone's poop on my hand. Do you do that; put poop on door handles because you don't wash your hands in here?"

Here are some things to try when you or the offender (or both) are about to leave the bathroom:

- 💩 When someone follows you out of the bathroom, grab the door handle and quickly pull your hand back and sniff your fingers. Then say, "*OH man, there's crap on the handle and it smells like you.*"

- 💩 Anytime someone wants to high-five, fist bump, or "tater" you, always ask the question, "*Did you wash?*" You can even say it under your breath like a subliminal advertisement. It's a bit passive aggressive but if you've done it enough times; people start to get the hint.

- 💩 "*Hey, did you use toilet paper in there? Why do that when you don't wash out here? You're a living oxymoron ... Sorry, I meant living fuckingmoron.*"

- 💩 When they start to leave without washing, you can simply tell them, "*Hey, you got some crap on your fingers, you're gonna wanna wash that, right?*"

- 💩 "*Whoa, that was a stinky crap you just left. Bravo! Imagine what your wiping hand must smell like.*"

- 💩 "*Check this out; I had pizza for lunch, went poop and now my fingers smell like poop and pizza. It's like one great taste and I think everyone should wash their hands after going poop.*" (Sure it doesn't make sense, but neither does not washing your hands after pooping. Am I getting through here?)

You get it; people don't wash their hands after pooping in the "men's" room. The reality is that if their own mother's couldn't teach them to wash, it's hard pressed that you'll ever teach them. So you should just vent your frustration by trying some of the things I've mentioned. At least you'll feel better and they'll feel insulted. High-five!

There you have the four rules of the Potty Protocol, but let's go through some example situations so you are fully prepared for what you might encounter. The following examples are of a standard bathroom with a layout that is pleasing and functional. You'll come across many different bathroom layouts but within your first five steps into any bathroom you should complete your assessment and determine exactly what your next action is. If you aren't sure, go ahead and ask someone at the urinal for a little help... NOT!

All bathrooms have different layouts offering challenges that need to be identified and resolved in just a few footsteps. You are bound to make mistakes and that's ok, but you need to be able to react quickly. The women's bathroom is a bit different in that they only have stalls and makeup counters and a make-out couch. I don't cover women's bathroom protocol because I'm not supposed to be in there. Chicks get to sit down to pee thus they don't have urinals so my diagrams and examples are only for the men's bathroom. OH, and for the women's bathroom, it's definitely ok to break rule number two and look each other in the eyes, if you're on the make-out couch...making out. And I know you are because I can see it in my head.

Now for the scenarios:
1. Read the description of the scenario.
2. Look at the picture.
3. Make your assessment what your action should be.
4. Check your answer in the "What do you do?" section.

Legend:
    The darkened urinal/stall is presently occupied
    The circled urinal/stall is the first and best option

Scenario 1:
Description: Two urinals occupied appropriately and you need to pee.

You've had six cups of coffee during a two hour meeting and you're not wearing adult diapers. If you hear one more person say, "synergy" or end their statements with "moving forward," you're liable to wet yourself on purpose just to cause commotion. You really need to pee, and when you enter this bathroom you find two urinals occupied and all stalls are open...

Scenario 1: Two Urinals Occupied

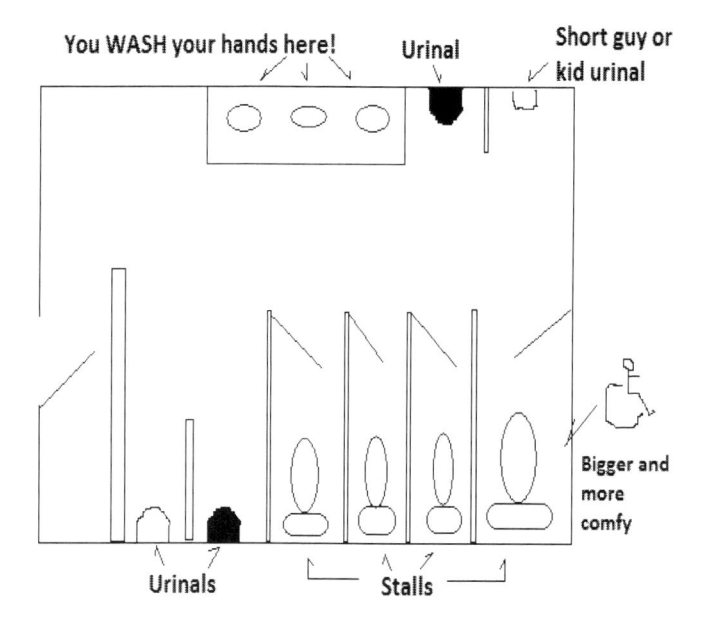

What do you do?

Smile. You're looking at an appropriate use of the restroom. But you're in a hurry, remember!? You've got to pee, NOW! The circled stall is the one you choose, but the handicap stall is an acceptable second choice.

Scenario 1 SOLUTION

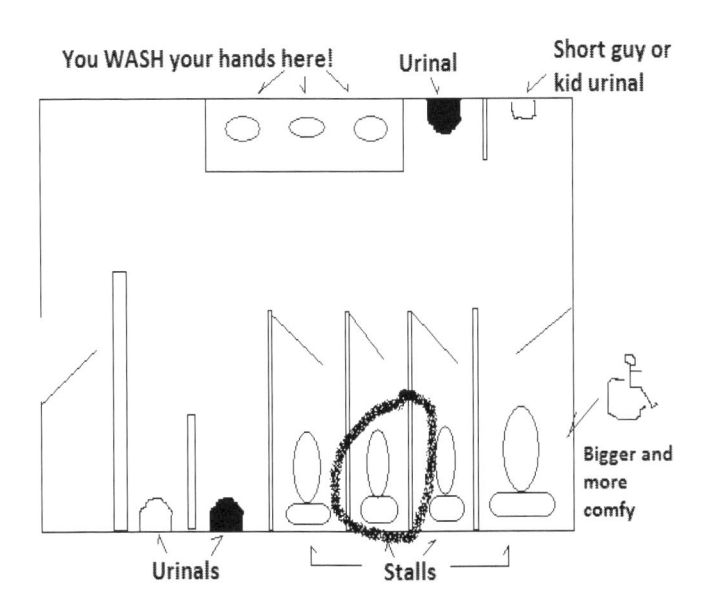

Diagram: Restroom layout showing "You WASH your hands here!" (sinks), "Urinal", "Short guy or kid urinal", "Urinals", "Stalls", and "Bigger and more comfy" (handicap stall). The middle stall is circled.

Why that one?

If you choose a urinal next to someone then you are breaking the third rule: Give a bro his space. If you stepped up next to one of those other guys, it would be awkward and uncomfortable. Why would you want to stand next to another man while both of you were holding penis' – penises? – peni?

Now you could be forced to use one of those urinals if the stalls were all full, but then that's acceptable because every man in that bathroom knows how many people are in there and what they're doing.

This can be a bit tricky, however, because your first thought might be:

"Why can't I just use the first open stall? There's a barrier between me and the next guy."

But you would still be next to another guy when you had <u>other</u> options. Taking the second stall or the handicap stall allows the next guy that comes in after you to make an appropriate choice; he'll know to take the one you didn't (the second or handicapped stall). This places at least one receptacle between you and anyone else. If a fourth guy enters the bathroom, he's screwed and should wait or go find another bathroom.

Last note on this, but it's incredibly important: In the above scenario where the two urinals are occupied and all stalls are open, you should <u>never</u> take the third open stall. The reason is because the next guy to come in has no alternative but to take a stall or urinal that is next to another guy. At best, he would have to choose the first stall which puts him next to the guy on the urinal. Any other choice puts him right next to someone – possibly you!

Scenario 2:

Description: Two stalls next to each other, both occupied and you need to poop.

You've been prairie-dogging a turd for twenty minutes waiting for your conference call to end. You've grabbed your magazine or fantasy baseball stats and need some "you" time. You race off to the bathroom without hanging up the phone only to open the door and quickly see that the first two stalls are occupied, the last two are open, and you've already started letting the dog out of its hole...

Scenario 2: Two stalls occupied

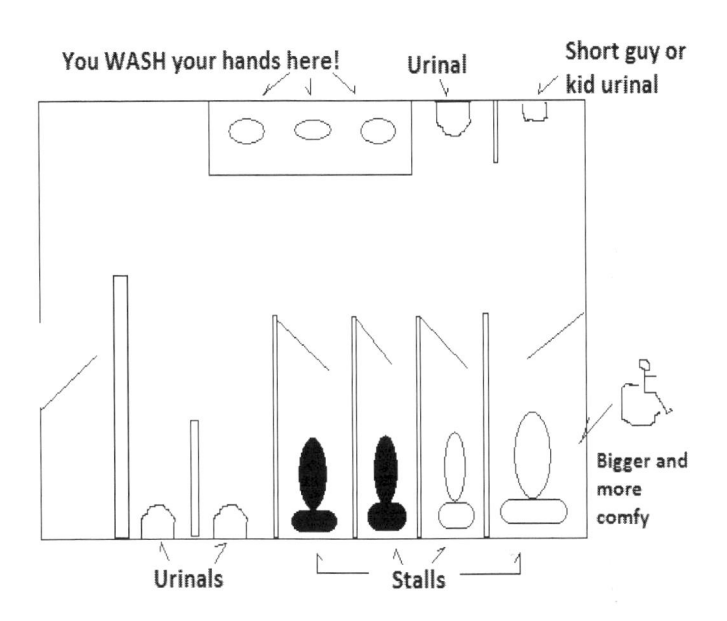

What do you do?
1. Assess the situation. Wow, this is a total breach of rule #3, "Give a bro his space." But you didn't do it and there is a chance these two idiots were forced into this situation based on who was in the bathroom when they came in. No matter, you can't concentrate on that, you're just a few moments away from having to throw

your underwear away if you don't make a quick decision!

2. Your obvious choice is to take the handicap or fat guy stall at the end. Sorry, that's not insensitive as much as it is a lack of being exposed to handicaps. Ok, maybe both of those comments are insensitive. But in my experience, that stall is typically used by fat people – and we had no dudes with wheels for legs so it was mostly available.

Scenario 2: SOLUTION

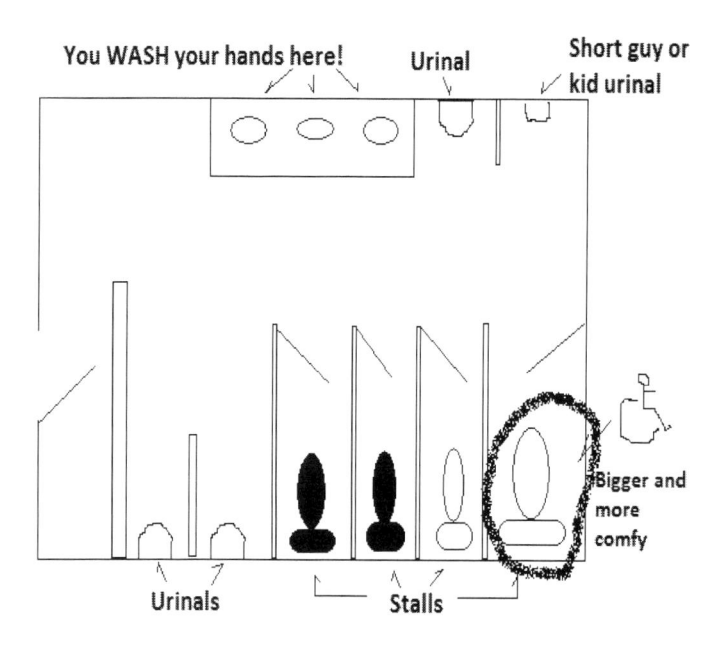

Why that one?
1. It's awkward to sit right next to another guy in most situations and always wrong to sit next to another guy while he purges his colon. It's also a blatant violation of the third rule – Give a bro his space. I repeat it so much because I care and it's SO IMPORTANT!

2. If you chose the third stall then you've just made a sandwich with three guys in a bathroom... Inappropriate.

3. You should always want to be as far away from another guy's stinky ass as possible.

4. This solution gives you comfortable space between you and other pooper's. However, it does serve up some risk of being in there when a handicap comes in. That's bad form on your part, but even the wheeled-guy should understand the protocol and just wait his turn by doing spins and those kick-ass wheelies they can do in their chair.

Scenario 3:

Description: Half of all stalls and urinals are occupied correctly.

You just downed three beers and four bean burritos from the taco truck for lunch earlier and they've all decided to leave your body – soon! You plow through the bathroom door to find this little gem: all urinals and stalls are occupied correctly. What is your exit strategy for your impending "exit strategy"?

Scenario 3: Stalls and Urinals occupied

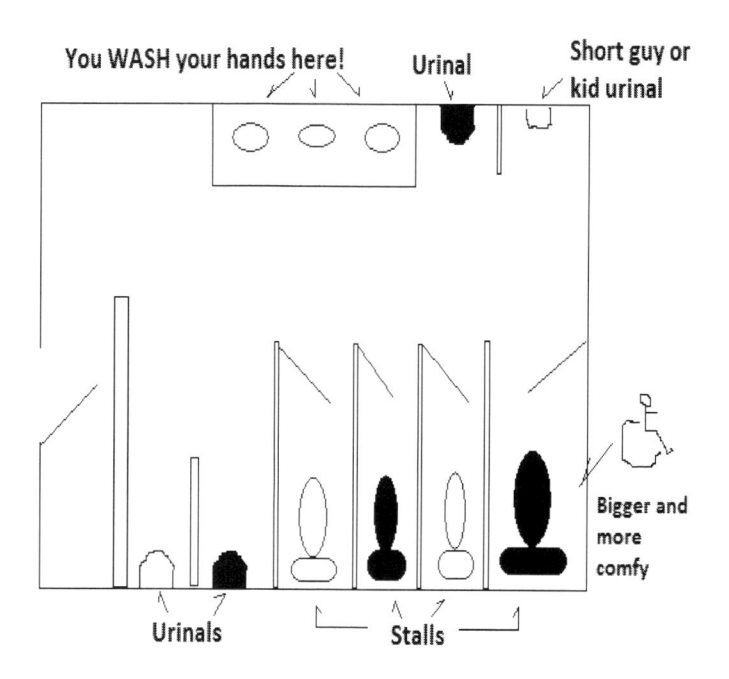

[Diagram of a bathroom layout with labels: "You WASH your hands here!" pointing to three sinks; "Urinal" pointing to an occupied urinal; "Short guy or kid urinal" pointing to a smaller urinal; "Urinals" labeling the row of urinals; "Stalls" labeling the row of stalls; "Bigger and more comfy" pointing to the rightmost stall.]

What do you do?

1. Since this scenario is at lunch time and at work, you have to simply find another bathroom.

2. If this were a club on a weekend, you'd drop trow and unload in the first sink on the left. Why that sink? Well, because it puts you facing the back of the guy at the urinal, and that's better than any other option here. If you chose the far right sink, you'd be facing the front of the guy in the second stall and you don't want to make stink-face at another dude. The middle sink might be fine, but in this bathroom layout, the far left sink is the

first sink to be seen by anyone else coming in and you want to make a bold statement that the bathroom is currently full. Seeing someone dump in a sink should always accomplish that.

3. In a pinch, you could take either stall but one of them is a better choice than the other…Care to guess? I'll tell you below.

Scenario 3: SOLUTION

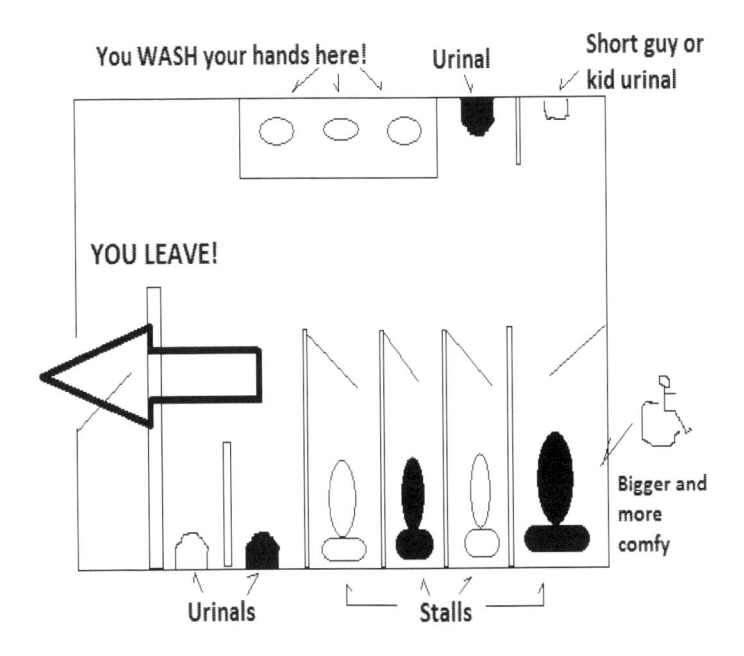

You WASH your hands here! *Urinal* *Short guy or kid urinal*

YOU LEAVE!

Bigger and more comfy

Urinals *Stalls*

Why that one?

1. You leave because you're honorable. You've recognized good bathroom etiquette and you're going to reward each one of these fella's by giving them their

93

privacy. Let the next douche bag bust in and break up this picture of beauty.

2. If you are at a club and you've been drinking, there's a good chance nobody is going to recognize or remember you. Also, in the layout provided, you can shit in the left most sink and still won't make eye contact with anyone – unless someone's peeping the stall cracks.

3. If you were in a pinch, did you guess the first stall or the third? If you chose the third stall, give back your man-card. The first stall is the obvious choice if you had no other bathroom choices or timing was not your friend. There are a few reasons why:

   - 💩 The odds are that the guy in the first urinal on the left is going to finish before the guy in stall #2, so you'll only have one dude to either side of you for a short while.

   - 💩 You should never plant yourself between two dudes having crap wars like the dudes in stalls #2 and #4.

   - 💩 You also don't want to sit and shit next to someone who is using the handicap stall unless forced to. There are many reasons for this but to name a few:
     1. He's handicapped and might be making handicapped sounds in there and that's disturbing.
     2. Handicapped people smell different.
     3. If it's a fat dude, fat dude's eat a lot and thus crap a lot and thus smell a lot which is reason enough.
     4. Because of the three reasons above there is significant risk of splash under when he

goes to wipe, stretch, stand up, roll away, or whatever. You don't want splash under from any stall, least of all from a handicapped or fat messy pooper.

Scenarios #4-7: Miscellaneous Scenarios

For the following scenarios I want to address miscellaneous situations that can happen in and out of the office. In my office bathroom experience over the years, the people that use them are generally the same people every day. That is, unless your turnover rate at your office is incredibly high, you are using the bathroom with the same people on a fairly regular basis. You may even share similar pooping schedules or at least know when not to go in after particular individuals. In addition, you probably have your favorite urinal and stall. Some of you may not even deviate from your favorites at any cost – even the cost of clean clothes for the remainder of the day.

So what happens outside the office? How can I prepare myself or practice good bathroom etiquette in other places I poop and pee? Great questions! Let's look at some situations you might find yourself in and ways you can deal with them effectively:

Miscellaneous Scenario 4: Sports Stadium

The following picture is a bathroom at a sports stadium. The scribbled "X" marks a user at the particular bathroom fixture. As you can see, all stalls are occupied and you don't want to ever go in a stall at a stadium. Since everyone knows you don't poop in a stadium bathroom because of potentially missing the big play, the guys that are in there must have had to go so bad that they decided to risk it. Always cut guys like that some slack, it might be you one day. Regardless, you know the stuff coming out of those stalls is not pretty and it's not somewhere you want to be. Leave 'em be.

The sinks are where we wash and since we are not at a dance club, you can't pee in the sink. Besides, too many dudes are trying to wash their hands and get back to the game. So that leaves you with just the urinals, which is fine because that's why you came in. Your quick assessment of the situation is this:

1. The first thing you notice is a short old man standing at the kid urinal – weird, but ok.
2. You also notice three people at each of the other urinals and all of them are in their early twenty's

Scenario 4: Sports Stadium

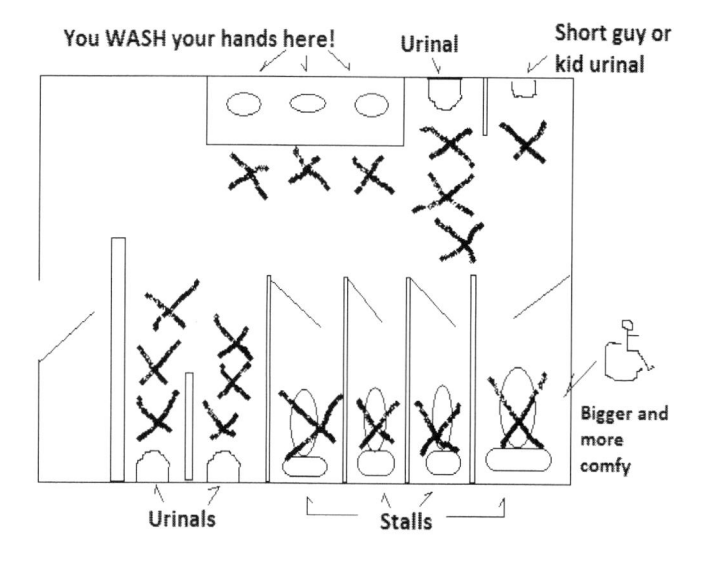

What do you do?

1. You're in luck; any of the urinals occupied by the twenty-something's is your best choice.

Why that one?

1. You might have thought it would be quicker to just jump in behind the one guy at the kid urinal. After all, it's only one guy and the other urinals all have three people. Your math is accurate, but your judgment is way off. Had you chosen to jump in behind the short seventy-year old at the kid urinal, you would have missed the second half, or the 5th inning, or matador goring or whatever it is you are supposed to be watching. Why? Because that dude's bladder is seventy years old and it takes him five times longer to pee than it does any twenty-year old. Those young dudes are going to piss so fast, you might not even have to break stride in the bathroom before a urinal opens up. Matter of fact, sometimes those guys will double up on a urinal saving all of us valuable time in there. Gotta love the youth!

2. Conversations. Remember, this is a stadium, not your office, so people are going to be chatting you up. Do you want to stand behind the old guy with the clogged catheter complaining about WWII and how he "saved PUKES like you" in the trenches? Or do you want to stand behind the young guys and listen to them argue each side of "fake vs. real" replete with details and phone-photo evidence from last night's activities? Chicks, man.

Miscellaneous Scenario 5: Camping

You've decided to take your sons camping in the woods at a state park "crampedground." You've pitched the tent, set up the sleeping bags, scrounged for wood and lit a fire. Now, you've cracked open the first of your twelve pack of cold ones, and got the hot dogs out and are waiting for good cooking coals – suddenly, your littlest man has to go poop.

You grab all of your boys because you know this thing is going to parlay into multiple trips if you don't, and head to the head...

Scenario 5: Camping

<Picture elided>

NO, you idiot! You're camping in the woods – state park or not – you take those kids into the forest and show them how to dig a hole and shit in the woods like a man. Because, yes, a bear does shit in the woods, and so should you! And if a tree falls and nobody's there, it still makes a freaking noise. You really gotta get your boys out and camp some more, Nancy.

Miscellaneous Scenario 6: Using the Women's Bathroom

Sometimes you'll find yourself in a situation where your only choice is to use the women's bathroom. The situation might be that there are only two bathrooms and they are unmarked on the outside, and they are identical in setup on the inside – like in small offices and some fast-food restaurants. Or perhaps the situation is that these are single stall bathrooms and the men's room is occupied and your bladder is quickly becoming your second largest organ. You enter the women's bathroom…

I've modified our previous bathroom picture to reflect a simpler, single user bathroom. I've added the make-out couch for completeness and accuracy. I've also removed the useless urinals and extra stalls for simplicity. There is just one sink, one stall, and the make-out couch.

Scenario 6: Using the Women's Bathroom

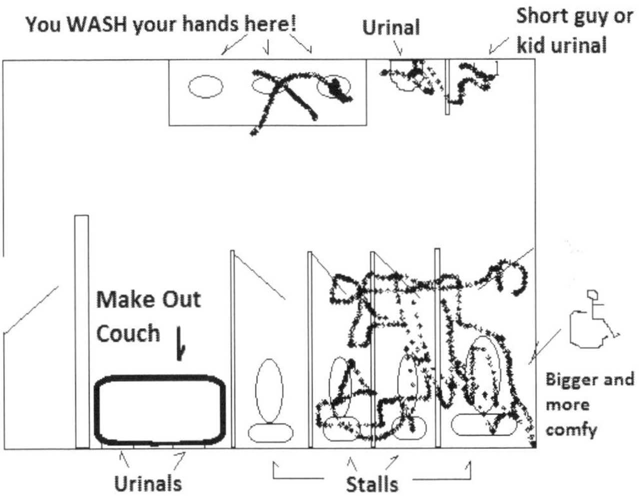
You WASH your hands here!
Urinal
Short guy or kid urinal
Make Out Couch
Bigger and more comfy
Urinals
Stalls

What do you do?

1. First (and I'm only saying this because I have to in order to keep the peace at home and the hate mail to

a minimum): You raise the lid before you pee and you close the lid after you pee.

2. There really isn't a second option on this. Don't mess with their seat; and if you do, clean it up.

Miscellaneous Scenario 7: Outhouses, Port-A-Potties

You will find yourself having to use a portable toilet at some time in your life. If you haven't, I highly recommend it so you can learn to appreciate the finer things in life – like pooping at home where your poop leaves the room that you are pooping in and goes outside somewhere. Portable toilets are disgusting by design. The people who maintain them don't want anybody hanging out in there and getting comfortable. They want you in and out so you have as little time as possible to create a mess. If portable toilets were clean and perfect, we'd just have them sitting in a corner of one of our rooms inside our house, rather than taking up an entire room just for pooping and peeing.

The situation: You're stuck in a traffic jam because a truck rolled over and you're three miles in either direction from an off-ramp. Lucky for you they're also doing road maintenance and the ground crew's portable toilet is on the other side of that Jersey-barrier over there. You need to go #2 so you get out of your mini-van, hop the barrier and get to the door…

Scenario 7: Outhouses, Port-A-Potties

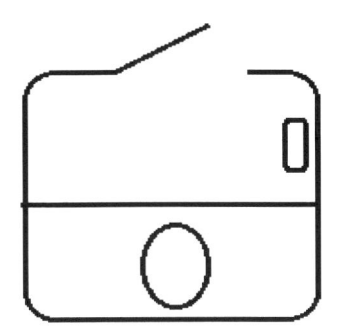

What do you do?

1. Don't touch anything. Literally, never touch anything on, around, or in these things.

2. You'll have to hover over the toilet hole. Construction workers are remarkably clean in that they don't like to sit on their shit any more than you do. But you still never know what's on that seat and if you approach all of them the same way, whether you've had good or bad experiences, you'll do just fine. Just hover your hole over this like it's a drop toilet. It takes a lot of leg strength because you won't be supporting yourself with your hands. Good luck!

3. Keep the level of the bowl water in mind. A short drop could cause unwanted splash up. If you're new to this experience, it's not as refreshing as a bidet or your regular bowl splash up, so be aware. The key is that there is a relation between the size of the turd and the distance to the water that determines the amount of splash up. Actually, here is a handy matrix:

Size of turd	Distance to water	Splash up risk
Small	Long	Lowest
Small	Short	Medium
Medium	Long	Medium to High, depending on turd entry
Medium	Short	Medium to High, depending on turd entry
Large	Long	High
Large	Short	Highest

💩 💩 💩

So there you have a number of scenarios to review and understand so that the next time you are faced with a bathroom situation, you can handle it. I hope the scenarios help you think along the right track next time you enter your bathroom at work or in the field. Sure, all bathrooms are different, but you have your daily routine bathroom and will be able to adapt pretty quickly with practice.

I've purposely left out the one-off scenarios like what to do when the bathroom employs a "Bathroom Attendant," or if the bathroom has only wall-less toilet stalls because those things are out of scope for most office situations. I can offer you this: You never shake the hand of a "Bathroom Attendant" and never use short-stalled toilets where you can see each other crap. You never want to see another man's shit-making-face – it haunts forever. If we all adhere to the Potty Protocol, all of our bathroom experiences will be what they were meant to be: comfortable, enjoyable, relaxing, safe, and clean.

Chapter 9:

Bathroom Babble

In chapter eight, on the Potty Protocol, rule #2 is: "Do not start any conversations." The emphasis was on not starting conversations but the fact is that you will find yourself in conversations, and even occasionally starting them in the bathroom. For those times when you do need to speak, there are a few things to keep in mind and a list of acceptable things to say and ways to say them. I've used the word "babble" in the chapter title for a reason. Remember this above everything else when communicating in a bathroom: Don't speak, but if you do, make it guttural, mean, and unintelligible babble.

Once again, this isn't necessarily new information to most men, but a lot of men still need to be told to wash their hands before leaving the bathroom so it's worth review. In this chapter I discuss some things you can say depending on where you are in the bathroom in relation to your target. Also, I finish with an in depth discussion regarding the "courtesy flush" and a rant about cell phone use in the crapper.

Speaking in the bathroom is nearly unavoidable. However, knowing what to say and how to say it can help avoid awkward situations for yourself and others. For example, it might be acceptable, but not encouraged, to walk into a bathroom and say simple, guttural words or phrases such as; "*Hey,*" "*Yo,*" "*'Sup?*" You can give a friendly head nod in another dude's direction but it is a bit suggestive in that it signifies you might want to start a conversation. So you have to be careful in what you say, how you say it, and who you say it to. You can sigh, spit, or groan or even a combination of all three, but never openly start a conversation unless provoked.

In this chapter, I've included a handy matrix to help you see the combinations of conversations. It cross references the four areas of the bathroom from where you might be speaking. Furthermore, the matrix includes the things you can say. It might be a little confusing to just look at the matrix and figure it out so let me start by explaining the self-explanatory so that I can be sure to be redundantly redundant:

1. **Coming in or going out**: This is the common area just as you enter or exit the bathroom where you have line of sight to most of the fixtures (sinks, urinals, stalls). Depending on the bathroom, this might be the first nine square feet or it might be five steps around a divider, but the one thing all coming in or going out areas have in common is that you are able to assess the current situations occurring at the sink, urinal, and the stalls.

2. **At the urinal**: This represents someone standing at a urinal.

3. **In a stall**: This represents someone inside a stall regardless of whether the stall door is closed or open or whether the person is sitting or standing.

4. **At the sink**: This represents someone standing at the sink

Before I get started on the matrix, I want to point out some personal tips that you can use to help yourself not break the rule of starting any conversations. Trust me, it was difficult to pull this topic out and make it into a separate chapter because I really believe the conversations should be minimal if at all. For instance, if I'm in a stall and you are in a nearby stall, I don't care if you run out of toilet paper or ass gaskets, you never say a freaking word. Just use your shirt to wipe your ass and tear it up and flush it – I don't care if it takes you three hours – you never speak to anyone anywhere when you are in a stall. It's that simple.

There is nothing you need to say in there that you can't say at the sink or in the lunch room or in email. If you sat down and <u>then</u> realized your roll was empty, that's poor ass – management and I just don't respect that. Helpful personal experience tip: you can take the cardboard toilet paper roll and tear pieces off and wipe your butt like scooping Fritos through bean dip. Yeah, it's disgusting, but you're gonna wash your hands afterwards, right?

Ok, I realize everyone is different, so although it is true that you should never talk in the bathroom, sometimes you might need to speak or even start a conversation. Like if someone is pissing on you or if they are on fire and don't notice it, you might need to speak for personal safety. But those are life threatening situations, and even then – sometimes, someone needs to jump on the grenade. I've beaten that enough… so let's just say that you do find yourself needing to speak in the bathroom. The following matrix will help guide you in what you can say to someone else depending on what you both are doing.

1. Find your position down the first column on the left.
2. The other person is at one of the places along the first row at the top.
3. Follow them until you meet somewhere in the matrix.

For example, if you are at the urinal and someone else is at the sink, you can't say anything to them (denoted by the

"X"). But if you are at the sink and someone else is at the sink, you can talk about chicks, sports or the weather... See for yourself, learn it, and then apply it.

	Coming/ Going	Sink	Urinal	Stall ***
Coming/ Going	"Hey"	"Hey"	X	X
Sink	"Hey"	Anything about: chicks, sports, or the weather- in that order.	X	"Courtesy flush?"
Urinal	X	X	X	"Courtesy flush?"
Stall ***	X	X	X	"Courtesy flush?"

*** = You should never speak nor be spoken to while in a stall. The "courtesy flush" request is a request I'm indifferent about and discuss in the next section.

If you follow these three bullets everyone will be happy and comfortable:

- 💩 If you don't start any conversations, it will eliminate nearly all communication and then nobody needs to remember the matrix.
- 💩 When both of you are at the sink or on your way out you are allowed to talk about chicks, sports, and/or the weather, but you don't have to talk at all.
- 💩 At the urinal or in a stall, nobody should be talking.

To courtesy flush or not to courtesy flush?

The courtesy flush is the act of flushing the toilet in an effort to squelch the stench as a courtesy to other bathroom visitors. The idea is that you flush what's currently in the bowl as a gesture of good will to let them know that, *"Hey, I'm stinking it up in here and I'm gonna clear the bowl out of courtesy to you. You're welcome."*

There are two types of courtesy flushes to discuss:

1. **Self-initiated** – You're in the stall and simply flush out of your usual rhythm because someone came into the bathroom.

2. **Requested** – Someone in the bathroom has violated the rule of starting any conversations and asked you to courtesy flush.

I'm not fully sold on the idea of utilizing the self-initiated courtesy flush. I don't feel it's appropriate or acceptable to initiate a courtesy flush out of the kindness of your heart, and here's why:

- I like my smell. My farts and poop are warm and comforting; it's part of my experience in there. If you don't like it, you can scoff and leave. I'll flush it after I'm done admiring it.

- If I courtesy flush for you it's like building an unspoken bond and we're both in the bathroom and one of us is naked – not cool.

- ♨ Most likely you won't do it for me so I won't do it for you. It's how I teach my kids: do unto others before they do it to you. It's in all the good parenting books.
- ♨ It's a non-verbal way of breaking the rule and starting a conversation. It's like I'm reaching out to you, saying, *"Come on in, it'll smell better, let's sit and chat."* Not gonna happen!

I don't agree with the requested courtesy flush either. I won't ask for one because I'm a man. You shouldn't ask for one because I'm a man. Not a typo. Don't ask me to flush my waste because your candy-cane nose is offended. If it's that bad, just throw some applause my way as you back out of the bathroom. Here are my reasons why I don't ask, and don't want to be asked, for a courtesy flush:

- ♨ It breaks rules #2 and #3 of the potty protocol – I've smelled ass gas that's coated my teeth before but I still won't break rule #2 by starting a conversation. On top of that, in a way, it's breaking rule #3 by invading a bro's space. You can applaud his efforts in there and/or make horrible sounding stink noises as you exit the bathroom, just don't say anything.
- ♨ It can be confusing – If there are multiple poopers in there and you haven't stated specifically, *"Hey, stall #2, dude with the flip-flops, courtesy flush please."* Then certainly confusion will start and that can disrupt someone's morning constitution and that's not cool. Let sleeping '<u>logs</u>' lie.
- ♨ Who goes into a men's bathroom expecting it to smell pretty? That's for the women's bathroom. I can't believe I'm saying this; but I want where I shit to smell like men.

💩 You don't know for sure what I'm doing in there; don't ask me to complete a task for you just because you've entered the bathroom. There's a good chance I might get mad and I'm not above flinging poo over the stall wall in your general direction.

So my answer to the question, *"To courtesy flush or not to courtesy flush?"* is that each pooper should use his discretion. I personally won't ask for one and might not respond in the way you expect me to if you ask me for one. Some cases, like when you're in there with a buddy, it might be ok to ask, but then you risk some serious repercussions from him and others. Golden rule: keep your mouth closed in the bathroom.

💩💩💩

Cell Phone Rant

Cell phone use is already impeding on valuable face-to-face communication by interrupting and becoming the primary focus of any conversation. If you're having a chat with another person and one of your phones ring, it's apparently ok if you answer that phone and shift the conversation focus to the person on the phone, effectively ignoring the person in front of you. It's rampant, it's rude, and it's a breakdown of communication and human contact that is desperately needed in this day and age. But worst of all: It's accepted.

Answering your cell phone is actually an expected reaction in today's world. The unknown phone call in your pocket suddenly becomes more important than <u>whatever</u> it is you were doing when you received the ring or vibration. And when the abuser learns that it's not an emergency on the other end of the line, the focus won't shift back to where it belongs, but if it does, it's already broken.

Granted, there are emergencies when a cell phone will save valuable time, but if you had one dollar for every time you used your cell phone for an emergency, I'd bet you'd have zero dollars – because contrary to what you've trained yourself to think of as an emergency; the fact that your twelve year old son had to walk home from school isn't an emergency, it's an adventure. Forgetting if you have milk at home and needing a cell phone to call and ask; is not an emergency – buy more milk.

Smart phones are a bit more helpful in that they can actually add content to a conversation. For example, you're chatting with a buddy about supermodels and you can't picture the face of that woman that was dating Tom Brady – BAM! Smart phone finds several pictures you and your buddy can use to refresh your memory. Or, let's say you and your buddy are stalking Tom Brady's supermodel girlfriend and you aren't entirely sure where to look – POW! Smart phone says, *"She's over there."* However cool it may be to have mobile porn, smart phones are still a disruptor.

But this is really about using the cell phone in the shitter. I clearly have issues with talking and being talked to in the bathroom. I have even more issues with some jackass making calls and/or taking calls while he's pooping. How does that affect me? I'll tell you: I have only one place where I am expected to relieve myself in private while at work. I can't poop in my office, I shouldn't be pooping in other people's offices, so the bathroom is the one place where I should be able to pee, poop, fart, hurl, and masturbate in private or semi-private – should the need arise.

Side note: I had another chapter on going #4, but I don't think the world is ready for my ground breaking idea for being more comfortable at work.

If you're on your phone telling your mother that her fudge brownies were awesome and that nobody can tenderize meat nor pull pork like she can, then I'm feeling a little uncomfortable. It's not fair...Not only to me, but to the person on the other end of the call. You should respect your mother more than that. I have the same feelings about someone walking into the bathroom on a current call. It's not a huge impact on me as I can finish anything anywhere at any time, but what about the person on the other end of the call? Do they know you just walked into a bathroom with them? You might argue that...

"But they can't see me when I'm in there."

I would argue that that is even worse than actually being there with you. For instance, if I am physically walking into a bathroom with you, I have an immediate reaction to what I can see, hear, smell, and even taste sometimes and my fight-or-flight instinct will take over. But if I'm on the other end of that phone with you and you walk into a bathroom, I only have my sense of hearing – but just like blind people, my sense of hearing is heightened when I can't see. So I am aware of where I am with you but will instantly form a much more negative picture in my mind as to what's going on around you and what you are doing or about to do. There is no way I'm focusing on the conversation we are having on the phone, I'm building disgusting events in my head and I'm not sure why. Even worse; you're going to talk to me like we aren't in a bathroom! That's just gross and wrong.

I'm courteous at work; I don't burp in meetings and I don't fart when I know other people might be around soon. So I take my farting to the only place I have sanctuary which is the bathroom or the semi-empty office on the third floor and sometimes the "rejuvenation room" ('cause I think that's funny). Guys go to the bathroom to scratch, sniff, fart, poop, pose, check our own package, primp, shave, brush teeth and hair, wash our hands (some of us), and to otherwise secure that we are all that is man. It's our individual private time with the understanding that there might be another dude (or dudes) in there with us, but that's unavoidable; but phone calls are avoidable. I can't understand why these ass-hats insist on answering or making calls on their cell phone in the poo room.

If I'm taking a dump and some guy walks in talking on his cell phone, it bugs the crap outta me – literally. It's not that I'm offended, but maybe I feel bad for the other person. Maybe I feel bad for the jackass that can't take three minutes to just piss and call them back. Regardless of the reason, I'm always prepared with a loud fart or burp. If I'm especially lucky I'll have eaten chili the previous day and can push out a huge growler during a quiet part of their conversation. However I can manage to accomplish it; if that dude hasn't identified to the person on the phone that he's in the shitter, I'm going to. Here are some things you can say to help stop the madness:

- "*Hey, dude, you got any toilet paper over there? I'm out and I got some serious hangers.*"
- "*Man, can you courtesy flush that stink? I know it's a shitter, but do you need to smell like that?*" (I'll break my own rules in these situations)
- If the "piss-phoner" and I are at the urinals, I'll look over and say loudly so the microphone picks it up, "*Hey, guy, it's $20 for the blow job and $60 for the blumpkin.*" (you might not wanna google "blumpkin" just accept that it's gross)
- "*Wow, it's true, you do have the smallest penis I've ever seen.*"
- "*Do you wipe with the same hand you dial with?*"
- "*Hey, ask her if she wants to come over and watch us pee.*"
- "*HEY CALLER! He's rubbing himself while talking to you! Don't be proud.*"

- 💩 "Hey dude, **condoms**? You should get your **condoms** at a drug store. Don't buy your **condoms** from that machine, it doesn't have any more **condoms**. Here, have one of my **condoms**."
- 💩 "Are you pooping and talking on the phone?"
- 💩 "Oh good, you brought your phone. Hook us up with that same girl as last time – it was only $100 each, right"
- 💩 "How's your herpes anyway? Did you ever tell her?"
- 💩 My personal favorite, which I've never had the balls to do: Just grab the phone out of their hand and say, "*Is that for me?*" Then just throw it in the urinal in front of you as hard as you can (without hitting your ding-a-ling) smashing it to bits. WARNING: This may be expensive and painful.

I realize my days are numbered as a "cell-phone-hater" because I'll soon have teenagers and will need to keep up with them. I guess I could still be a hater and use one, but I'm going to hold out as long as I can because I really don't see a need for them other than for playing. I think we can all be a lot more courteous with the use of cell phones and continue to build strong relationships with the people who are physically around us. If none of the people around you like you very much, go ahead and call a "friend," or fake like you have one.

So there you have the things you can say in the bathroom and where it's somewhat appropriate. But the bottom line is that if you just don't say anything, you don't have to worry about upsetting the flow and function of the bathroom. We all have to get along in there and we're all doing roughly the same thing, so be courteous of your fellow poopers. Like my dad used to tell us, "*Keep your mouth shut or someone's going to close it for you or put poop in it.*" Not sure that really applies here, though. I used to think it meant something similar to putting your foot in your mouth, like when you've said something stupid – but it didn't. It meant exactly what he said.

He was a troubled man.

💩 💩 💩

I shared my personal flavor on the courtesy flush and that we just don't need them. I also gave you my opinion on cell phones and how they are ruining interpersonal relationships, and I provided you with things to say to punks on the phone in the pisser. Just relax in the bathroom and do your business, nobody is going to thank you for doing it right, but they will point out when you've done it wrong, and you don't want anyone telling you how to poop…And yet, here I am.

Chapter 10:

Paid to Poop

Pooping is like many things in our lives: we take it for granted. You probably haven't put as much thought into pooping as I have, but if you did, you'd soon realize that it's quite possibly the best part of your day. It's really the only "you" time and for the most part it's relaxing, rewarding, and accompanied by relief. It's the "Three R's" you weren't taught in grade school. You'd be hard pressed to find another three to thirty minute activity that offered you the same benefits.

Granted, pooping in the comfort of your favorite bathroom provides the best opportunity for success, but at work you can find comfort in realizing that you are getting paid to poop. Companies understand that if they had you clock out every time you had to poop, you'd become disgruntled, unhealthy, and may even start pooping in your own office. I've done it, the precedence has been set. But don't let it get to that.

It's important to understand that this is a perk for working at your company. You're not going to find it printed in any employee manual or in an office memo; it's just an accepted form of compensation that no one talks about. It's not in your benefits package or discussed at review time. But don't think of it like you do with the free paper, pens, and use of the copier for personal copying; that's actually stealing.

And it's not just for blue collar office workers either; everyone who has ever received a paycheck from a job understands the idea of getting paid while making doody. We've all sat down on a seat and started squeezing and thought about the fact that our employer is currently paying us to make in the toilet. Pooping itself is rewarding, comforting, and fulfilling, but when accompanied by a paycheck, that's when it all comes together. Isn't it the little things in life that are so grand?

But it wasn't always this way. Years ago, you had to do your business on your own time, not during company work hours. This meant you would have to take your coffee break and fit in a growler on the john, all within ten minutes. It was never relaxing and you certainly didn't have time for anything else in there. Nobody was going to pay anyone for pooping. However, labor laws were developed, owners of companies realized this was silly so they started loosening up. But that has only happened within the last one hundred years or so; people have been working and pooping for thousands and thousands of years. So when did getting paid to poop really start?

I think we have to go back to the first people to make poop. Most likely some Neanderthal dude about 100,000 years ago made poop in the cave where everyone sat and ate Mammoth meat. Cak and Ug and several other Homo's (that's short for "Homo Sapiens" and perfectly acceptable) sat around their cave chewing when Ug crapped himself in the same spot he did the night before:

Cak: *"Ug, you outside, make pile."*

Ug: *"Ug."*

Even though everyone in the cave smelled like ass, the stuff under Ug made them sick. Ug always obliged and went outside to poop or rub off what was left on the softest rock he could find. Each night at dinner, (I'm making an assumption that eating Mammoth meat, grass, and dirt makes for regular bowel movements), Ug would make where he sat and the others would tell him to leave.

Cak: *"Ug, you outside, make pile."*
Ug: *"Ug, ug."*

Having no brain mass for memory, this went on for a few weeks or more, each night like the one before. Finally, Cak led the brain trust with a revolutionary idea; <u>before</u> sitting down to serve the Mammoth meat – pay Ug to go poop!

Cak: *"Ug, you outside, make pile. Not sit here."*
Ug: *"Ug."*
Cak: *"Before go. Take extra leg. You gnaw. You take time."*

Ug said nothing, he took the leg, went outside and enjoyed the first ever payment for pooping. Every night he forgot just like everyone else so it was a new experience and a lasting source of extra income in the form of more food for Ug.

Before too long, everyone wanted to enjoy extra legs while doing what they had to do anyway. Whining ensued, cavemen and cavewomen argued and shook sticks at each other. Soon, resentment would build up in generations of people, there were beatings, and eventually unions were formed. Then workers' rights improved while the quality of products and productivity of people didn't. And here we are – I've written a book about getting paid to poop and you've purchased it. We're good people.

We really haven't evolved a whole lot from that first moment with respect to pooping at work. I'm pretty content with my one poop a day routine. The feeling comes about the same time every day and I know in about seven minutes I'm going to be resting, pooping, and getting paid the same amount I got yesterday for pooping. In fact, I'm getting paid the same amount for pooping as I do for testing diacritic alias names for SMTP addresses over Telnet sessions. Both tasks are work, but pooping is warm and comforting and I get to be naked. But there are times when my "per-poop-price" (PPP) steps up a notch or two: like May 6th and 7th. I love Cinco de Mayo!

But there are some guys at my work that routinely poop two or three times a day (*yes, a guy will share that with another guy but then have a hard time telling his wife she's pretty – but yet have no problem telling the bikini-barista she has nice thighs and tats. We're complicated*). I suppose you could take an extra trip or two a day and fake it in there. Management shouldn't really gripe as long as you're doing it in the designated location.

However, management does still get involved sometimes. It started for a friend of mine at another office when he realized that some guys were excessively pooping, as much as four times a day! That's a seriously inflated PPP, so he took it upon himself to go to the bathroom five times a day. At just ten minutes a trip that would be nearly an hour of paid pooping. That's embezzlement! … And it didn't go unnoticed either. Following is a memo he received from HR:

"Jib, although we appreciate your hygiene efforts for your health and others in the office, we have noticed an increase in your bathroom visit activity over the last couple of months. We would appreciate it if you would take one or two of those jobs per day home with you. We've arranged a meeting between you and your manager to discuss, please attend. Thank you."

Manager: *"Hi Jib, I'd like to get right to the point of this meeting and this isn't going to be comfortable for either one of us, I'm sorry to say."*

Jib: *"I'm fired again, aren't I?"*

Manager: *"No, no, it's not that.... We've just noticed ... Well there's been some talk about the number of times you use the facilities in a given day and we feel it might be impacting your productivity."*

Jib: *"Are you talking about the bathroom?"*

Manager: *"Yes, that's right, we think you might be taking extra breaks and we just want to be sure you're ok."*

Jib: *"Are you guys watching me when I crap?"*

Manager: *"Absolutely not! We just casually noticed that your bathroom breaks have increased over the last couple of months and we wanted to make sure you were feeling ok."*

Jib: *"I'm fine, I just get raging turds that I can't pull the reigns back on and I can only prairie-dog 'em for so long."*

Manager: *"Ok, ok, we just want to make sure your health is in check and that your productivity remains at a comparable level to other engineers in the department."*

Jib: *"Oh, so you want to make sure that I'm producing the same number of growlers as other engineers in …"*

Manager: *"NO, no, I'm not being clear enough… We would like you to monitor your bathroom breaks and not allow them to interfere with your productivity."*

Jib: *"But it seems <u>you</u> are monitoring my bathroom breaks and it <u>is</u> interfering with my productivity – I'm not pooping or working right now. Perhaps we should make a Gantt chart and track my progress. I can go add a User Story, 'course that's gonna change my backlog – I said, "backlog"…"*

Manager: *"Please, that won't be necessary."*

Jib: *"We could color code it to designate patterns in consistency and color – whether it's a floater or sinker, steam or no steam…"*

Manager: "*Please leave.*"

Jib: "*Do you have any more ass-gaskets? My favorite stall is out and it says right on the empty box, "Provided for your protection by the management*"

Manager: "*Get out!*"

My friend had some serious issues with authority and he's not the most reliable guy so take that story with a grain of salt. I think the point is that you shouldn't mess with your poo routine out of jealousy of someone else's. Sure, we all get envious when a buddy calls you into the stall to check out his photo worthy log. But you shouldn't make it a contest – one of you is liable to blow your sphincter and then you won't be controlling anything down there. You're best to stick with your usual routine and try to increase your paid to poop value by being more productive in the bathroom.

I'm nothing if not helpful, so in a little bit I'll provide some suggestions to help you get started on your bathroom multitasking. I'm not an authority on what people do at work or even what work is, but I'm sure there are some things in your daily life that can also be done while pooping. Think "Angry Birds," magazine reading, primping, coloring, self-tattoos, stretches, etc. Anything that is personal and quiet in there. Keep to yourself. Just be careful not to create commotion or raise awareness of yourself in there. Somebody might think you're trying to start a conversation.

I know the following suggestions are going to contradict some of my own rules and what I just said about keeping to yourself. I'm even going to sound relatively hypocritical when I tell you to talk in the bathroom or use your cell phone in there. But I'm trying to provide you with other avenues for being productive. And they might even sound a little far-fetched, as if there is no way anyone would actually do these things. I've witnessed some of these things happening, but that doesn't mean you should, it's just more opportunities to think about.

So just keep in mind that the following ideas are effective ways to be more productive, but there's a tradeoff in that you'll have to break some rules.

💩 **Water cooler conversations**: If you are shooting the breeze with a co-worker around the office water cooler, you are wasting their valuable time as well as the company's money. Softly interject the idea that the group take this conversation up in the privacy of the stalled walls in the bathroom. You can enjoy the same conversation while comfortably pooping. Meanwhile, you are earning a paycheck, relaxing, and it's perfectly acceptable and encouraged by management.

Example: Jib, Sally, and Derek sip cool water from the company paid filtered water cooler...

Jib: *"Sup, Sally? – Derek, you're rockin' that tie dude – bringin' the bow back?"*

Sally: *"I'm fine."*

Derek: *"Yeah, that's funny, Jib...You working today? Thought you had administrative leave?"*

Jib: *"Naw, that was over yesterday...but I am off tomorrow for the court date."*

Sally: *"Yeah, sorry to hear about that Jib, if it's any consolation I do think I have a nice chest, some people might just be too sensitive about that stuff when it's said during a presentation."*

Jib: *"Whatevs ... I said it and I meant it. Hey, whattya guys say we take this convo into the bathroom and kill two birds with one load? I'm supposed to be more productive and this way we won't be wasting too much company time."*

Sally: *"I'm a girl."*

Derek: *"Actually, that's a good idea, I had Spam for breakfast."*

Jib: *"Let's roll. See ya, Sally."*

▲ **Doorway discussions:** Even coffee breaks can cause scorn from non-coffee drinking co-workers. As you and your buddy sip your "sin-syrup" in an office doorway, inevitably someone will walk by and scowl at you and hope you choke. Solution: take your mugs into the poo-room and be heralded for combining your coffee break with a shared poo, thus saving the company money. Here's an example where Jib and Billy are in the middle of a conversation in Billy's office enjoying their morning brew...

> **Jib:** *"...I mean SMOKIN' hot, dude."*
>
> **Billy:** *"Behind you ..."*
>
> <<Jib turns to see Clark standing just outside the door, arms folded>>
>
> **Clark:** *"Why don't you guys close your door, or better yet: GET TO WORK!"*
>
> **Jib:** *"Whoa, dude, chillax, we're just chattin' 'bout Sally and her bodacious ta-ta's."*
>
> **Billy:** *"I wasn't."*
>
> **Clark:** *"Jib, it's that kinda stuff that got you in trouble the last time. I'm going to have to report you."*
>
> **Jib:** *"Nobody likes you, Clark."*
>
> **Billy:** *"I do."*
>
> **Clark:** *"I don't care, Jib! At least I work around here."*
>
> **Jib:** *"You aren't working right now, and in fact are wasting our time. Billy, whattya say we go finish our coffee in the can? Mine's already made its way through my system and I need to go drop a Clark."*

<<Jib edges past Clark and heads down the hallway>>

Clark: *"Very funny, you're gonna be fired."*

Jib: *"At least people like me."*

Billy: *"They don't."*

💩 **Cell phone business:** Some of your real business might be accomplished while doing your "business." Cell phone calls are popular in poopers now, as one out of eight people use their cell phone in the bathroom based on a made up survey – and those are just the ones I'm in there to see. Let's say you need to make an important business phone call and driving and talking is illegal in some states. Take your business to the bathroom with you. The "poop-n-chat" is gaining popularity, much to some people's disdain (including this author):

Here's an example: Jib needs to place an important phone call in order to close the deal, but it's May 6th and he's been spending more time than usual in his cubicle – and I'm not talking about his work space. So he takes his call with him to the bathroom before it's too late. We catch up with Jib as he's finishing up the call and the push…

Jib: *"…it'll have to make 16%, any lower and I'm not making any money."*

Caller: <however you would spell the sound Charlie Brown's teacher makes on the phone – imagine that here>

Jib: *"Ok, ok. Let's try this: Keep the price the same, I'll throw in delivery, and next week I'll bring your* *team lunch on Monday, Wednesday, and Friday. But next month we'll...Hold on for a minute will you, Frank?"*

<<Holds the phone against his chest and speaks over the stall wall>>

"Hey buddy, you have any toilet paper over there? I'm dry over here; can you roll a roll over? Thanks.

<<Phone back to ear, continues call with Frank>>

"Frank, you still there? Good, so can we finish this up? Next month we'll sweeten the deal, I'm tired of being your number two." ...

- 💩 **Weekly one-on-one discussions with your manager:** I think you'll agree that holding discussions with your manager while you are both pooping will be more productive because the frequency at which you'll have these discussions will diminish. Added bonus: the amount of time discussing anything will be next to nothing.

    Nobody wants to talk while pooping and in fact getting your manager to agree to this is the difficult part – and I'd add a bit disturbing if s/he does agree. But that doesn't matter because if this isn't believable then I wouldn't be writing it, correct? So work with me for a minute, you've come this far.

    Ok, it's been a couple of weeks since the last meeting with your manager and although those previous meetings took place in the bathroom, they still went rather well, so this one should be fine...

Manager: *"Hey Jib, it's probably time for another one-on-one, do you have anything to discuss?"*

Jib: *"Nope."*

Did you see that? The power of whether they even have a meeting shifted to the employee – I'm telling you, there's power in pooping! The manager is doing what he is supposed to: checking in with his report to see if there is anything on his mind. We know he doesn't want to do it in the bathroom, but he wants to empower the employee in his career aspirations and part of that empowerment is being in control of his time and the management of that time. The manager has *asked* Jib if there is anything to discuss because he doesn't really want to do it in the bathroom. By asking, he's freed himself of any obligation should Jib say no.

However, they do have to meet on occasion to keep the lines of communication open. Here's an example of an actual meeting taking place in the bathroom…

Manager: *"So, I don't really have anything and I'm a little uncomfortable with your chosen meeting format."*

Jib: *"Shhhh. You're making it creep back in. Let's just get past breaking the seal down there and then we can talk. Grrrrrr"*

Manager: *"That's it, I'm outta here."*

Jib: *"Wait—Can I have a raise?"*

Manager: *"We'll discuss later, I'll swing by."*

Jib: *"Toilet paper?"*

There we have an effective meeting complete with the setting of discussion points for the next meeting – and it looks like someone's getting a salary adjustment!

Think of your daily routine, are there things you might be able to accomplish while pooping – in addition to pooping? I like to think about my family's finances while on the pot. I'll lay logs and lament having to pay for my kids' college credits now when I'm not fully certain janitorial services are taught at an accredited school. I'll pop pimples on my thigh and self-check my testicles – sometimes for cancer, but mostly for elasticity and fun. If there were a mirror on the back of the door I'd check out my poop face because I don't think I've ever seen the real one. Sure, I've practiced in front of a mirror before, but I wasn't actually pooping so it was a little forced and faked. I'd like to see the real deal sometime. The point is: there are a lot of different things you can do while pooping, you might think of some things you could get done or perhaps you just want to enjoy your little slice of "you" time by sitting quietly.

Pooping is an excellent thing to do at work and it's a part of the day that is just for you so use it how you want. If that means multitasking then great! If it means soaking in some relaxing vapors and enjoying the peace of the moment, then that's great too! If you currently view your poo time as inconvenient or something that you just have to do – change your tone. Pooping is something you <u>get</u> to do, get out there and enjoy it…And save some for work time, they'll pay you to do it.

Chapter 11:

The End

I've worked very little to provide you with ways to make your office job more enjoyable. I've shown you how to interview effectively (if not illegally) and even provided an example of an interview I went on so you can be cool too. With my APE approach, you should be on your way to securing your place in interviewing history.

I've discussed many different jobs for you to apply for that should fit any skill level – you just need to decide what's difficult and how heavily you want to disappoint your prospective employer. I've helped you understand the need for less acronyms and more pretty people in the work force. And I've provided you with how to communicate via email to ensure you do as little work as possible. I even threw in a topic about texting and showed you how to stalk under the guise of "research." Finally, I've addressed the bathroom and what the proper behavior is in that room with respect to how to handle your business in a proper and acceptable manner.

Life is really short and you're going to have to work for most of it so make it fun. I sincerely hope you enjoyed my attempt at crude humor and that nobody was hurt by any of it. Work doesn't come easy for me so I try to make it fun, otherwise I'd probably be sad, frustrated, and upset all the time. I wouldn't wish that state of life on anyone.

Most of us have to work to make a living for ourselves and our family. If you can't find something fun about the job you have, find a way to make it fun for yourself. You'll come home happier and healthier and your family will appreciate it.

Made in the USA
Lexington, KY
16 December 2015